White Scars

White Scars

On reading and rites of passage

Denis Hirson

Jayne
A book about books for someone
who is engaged in the generosity
of sharing the pleasure of reading
With warm wishes,
Denis Hirson
Johannesburg,
August 2006

JACANA

First published in 2006 by
Jacana Media (Pty) Ltd

Jacana Media (Pty) Ltd
10 Orange Street
Sunnyside
Auckland Park 2092
South Africa
(+27 11) 628-3200
www.jacana.co.za

ISBN 1-77009-256-0
978-1-77009-256-3

Set in Ehrhardt 11/14pt
Printed by Paarl Print

CONTENTS

INTRODUCTION

SURROUNDED

White Scars takes as its starting point four books, each of which I once needed to read over and over, to the point of obsession. The longer I have thought about my relationship with these books, the stranger it has appeared to be, and the more I have wanted to investigate it.

Why, for example, at the age of thirteen, should I have sat cross-legged on the floor of our Johannesburg house, repeatedly scrutinizing the black and white photographs of a massacre?

Ten years later, far from the suffocating atmosphere of apartheid South Africa, in the middle of exotic, disorienting Paris, why should I have found myself relentlessly toiling over a book of poems in Afrikaans? For me, this language had been nothing but a leaden drudge at school and then in the army, a source of pestilence in South Africa at large.

Then, after being attracted for several decades to dense, lyrical language, why was it that for almost a year, quite literally the only book I was able to read contained poetry of simple, sometimes even rough-shod directness?

Lastly, why should I have been attracted to a French book listing 479 apparently impersonal, banal memories, most of which I did not share and many of which I did not even understand?

With hindsight, these books all seem to be a little anomalous. And though each of them came to be significant to me, their promise was so well hidden when I first picked them up that I failed to read any of them through to the end.

It was not the words of Ambrose Reeves' *Shooting at Sharpeville* which interested me at all, but the photographs appended to the text. In the case of Breyten Breytenbach's *Die Ysterkoei Moet Sweet* (The Iron Cow Must Sweat), I could barely understand the language in which the book was written. Raymond Carver's *In a Marine Light* hardly elicited in me what the French would call "un coup de foudre", an instant lightning flash of passion. And when it came to Georges Perec's *Je me souviens* (I remember), the content initially seemed so alien to me that I only returned to it more than ten years later.

Yet in the end these books did not simply interest me; they surrounded me. This, it seems, was due not only to the books themselves, but to a feeling of resonance, or on the contrary a telling dissonance, between what I found in them and the circumstances of my life at the time. So in the following pages I juxtapose fragments of text about the books and fragments of autobiography, hoping that each might throw some light on the other.

THE DEMURE WAR ZONE

I left South Africa with my family at the end of 1973, when my father, who had been a political prisoner, was released. Seven or eight years later, I started writing *The House Next Door to Africa*, a series of dense prose fragments primarily concerned with autobiographical memory, opening with some ancestral tales and ending with our family about to set off from Johannesburg for Europe. That book was first published in 1986, when the white regime was still viciously holding its own.

Writing about apartheid South Africa at the beginning of the twenty-first century, given the changes the country has undergone in the past two decades, is a very different matter. The further away I move from life as I remember living it under apartheid, the less likely that life appears to be.

South Africa in the decades following the Second World War, though it might have come to seem immutably normal to many of its inmates, was a place of deceptive tranquility. In 1948, ex-servicemen only recently back from the front found themselves faced with a National Party government many of whose members had been openly pro-Nazi, and whose belligerent policies promised anything but peace.

As early as 1951, Bartho Smit, in his prescient short story "I Take Back my Country," has a black protagonist informing a white acquaintance that his people have taken to engaging in resistance:

> They slip quietly about you in the dark, stealing your property, raping your women, murdering. You think we don't know what we're about. But we know only too well we are making you afraid. We want you to become like small children in the darkness of this country [...][1]

[1] In Hirson with Trump (eds.), *The Heinemann Book of South African Short Stories*, p.140, tr. from the Afrikaans by Catherine Knox and Martin Trump

In the years following the publication of Smit's story, and particularly after the Sharpeville massacre of March 21st 1960, fear and repression lined the fabric of everyday life, particularly black everyday life. And yet this was apparently imperceptible to most residents of the white northern suburbs of Johannesburg where I was living at the time. Who had the slightest inclination to see beyond the servants with subdued eyes in starched livery in the mansions, and wild delight from the swimming pools outside?

In these demure surroundings, life was conducted from behind invisible trenches of nonchalance and over-politeness. Perhaps the extreme normality of it all was the clearest sign of the fact that there was a war going on in the country. Its visible incidents were dispersed across several decades, and often out of sight of most whites; its effects were incremental: a slow-fused, low-tension, feudal war of waiting.

Intermittent signs of violence did jut through the well-ordered surface of everyday life: burglaries, maddened dogs at gates, police-raids for blacks without passes. And there were more subtle, sadistic battles going on. Any morning of the week one could wake up to see "dustbin boys" hitching steel bins to their shoulders and pounding tackies into the tar trying to catch up with the white truck driver, who was always one jasmine-sweet block further ahead.

Sometimes the poison of inhumanity, like the act of resistance, was lodged only in the smallest word or gesture. Those critically minded whites who could see what was happening were ill at ease; those who named it publicly were branded as traitors. The comfort of the suburbs was sealed in a constantly maintained, highly political silence. It was not in the material interest of whites to break this seal. Neither did the blacks do so, seemingly held back by sheer powerlessness, combined with a habit of forbearance.

GRAFTING WORDS ONTO THE ROOT OF SILENCE

In my own case, the ambient silence was multiplied by a state of inner turbulence that came with the absence of my father. I experienced an inability, or refusal, to express verbally what I was going through both personally and in the world around me. It is no accident that the first book I write about here, *Shooting at Sharpeville*, is one that I initially became involved in as a young adolescent without reading a single sentence of the text.

Writing *White Scars* has meant finding words for a time when my own words would not come to me. It has meant returning to the boy, the adolescent, the young man I once was, and delivering to them from out of this distant present a parcel of language so that they might in turn speak back to me.

While reading about Raymond Carver's poetry, I came across a statement which helped me think about this process :

> Jeanne, a disciple of Karl Jaspers, taught me the philosophy of freedom, which consists in being aware that a choice made now, today, projects itself backwards and changes our past actions.[2]

I take this to open the possibility of re-imagining, or as Stephen Rose puts it, "re-membering"[3] the past by tapping energies that were once locked there by force of circumstance. This has resulted in the impression of almost being able to alter, retroactively, the sense of dumbness which once invaded me.

Likewise, but on a very different plane, this book goes back not only to my own experience but to the work of various writers in apartheid South Africa. With the exception of some poetry and plays, I was virtually ignorant of such work when I left the country as a young adult, and only made up for this lack much later, in the years following Nelson Mandela's release. If I have referred to South African texts from beginning to end here, it is both to insert them, as it were, into my previous world, and use them as a sounding board for later experience.

FREIGHT

While working on this book, I found myself using certain words which I had invested with a fairly heavy but not necessarily explicit freight of meaning. In some cases, these words also contained a

[2] Tess Gallagher's introduction to Carver's *A New Path to the Waterfall*, p.315. The statement is by Czeslaw Milosz.

[3] *The Making of Memory*, p.104

high charge of emotion. Inspired by Raymond Williams' book, *Keywords*, and particularly by his understanding of the way in which historical and ideological contexts inform the use of words, I thought it would be useful to extract and look more closely at them.

Each word I chose seemed to suggest a different line of approach, sometimes leading to questions of etymology, or personal association, sometimes to the use made of a word by or about a particular writer, which might in turn provide insight into this writer's world.

The largest group of words, including "township", "pass", "Jim", "baas", "island", "pylon", "underground", "anthem" and "voice", is specifically connected in my mind with apartheid South Africa. Many words in this group are to be found in the inventories, here called "Wordkeys", appended to each of the first two parts of this book.

A second group of words, including "corridor", "expat", "unsettler", "elsewhere", "refugee", "exile" and "Russia", is taken up in the "Wordkeys" section following the third and fourth parts of this book, and is clustered around the experience of uprooting.

The smallest group of words, scattered throughout *White Scars*, is shot through with the above preoccupations, but also touches on more literary and or existential questions. This group includes "banal", "purity", "artifice", "rite of passage" and "nomad".

In general, many of the words I have chosen concern the human organization of space, as well as displacement from and movement through space. In *White Scars* as a whole, I have traced a kind of geographical and linguistic spiral, with the initial, tightly constrained South African context at its base, constantly returned to and re-evaluated in the light of later, wider circles of experience of the world and the word.

W/RITES

I became engrossed in the *Shooting at Sharpeville* photographs in the wake of my father's arrest, round about my thirteenth birthday. *Die Ysterkoei Moet Sweet* took up my energy as a reader and then translator soon after I arrived in France, in the mid-1970's. It was my father's death which led me back to reading *In a Marine Light* as if for the first time; *Je me souviens* preoccupied me as I was emerging from a period of mourning for him.

Puberty and deep loss; arrival on an unknown shore, later to become my home; the witnessing of death and the experience of mourning: each of the books I have chosen here entered my life during a time of radical transition, a personal rite of passage.

Discussing initiation, the anthropologist Victor Turner describes a liminal state, " 'a moment in and out of time', and in and out of secular structure" during which the initiate's being is rendered malleable as the clay with which his body has been literally or figuratively daubed.[4]

This, in one way or another, corresponds to the period when I read the four books I want to speak of here. At each point, I was stripped of a deep physical bond with a person or place, finding myself in that state of vulnerability which marks the threshold of change.

In such a state, the limits of the self become more liquid, the spirit more receptive, and habit less blinding. "To be vulnerable is to be fully human" says Antjie Krog, "it is the only way you can bleed into other people".[5]

But vulnerability is also a state in which one might be tempted to retract into oneself, in response to the raw emotion of loss, the feeling of uneasiness in the face of the unknown. Perfect circumstances under which to turn to a book whose powers can be quietly distilled in solitude, in one's own time, the page both a screen for the spirit and a source of meaning, a map.

TONGUES

The books I have chosen here were written in three different languages, English, Afrikaans and French.

Breyten Breytenbach writes in Afrikaans, the official language of apartheid, armoured with puritan value and oppressive purpose, or, as he himself puts it, "a fulsome Germanic strain of throat-terrorism".[6] When I came to decipher what he was saying, I was

---

[4] *The Ritual Process*, p.82
[5] Untitled film interview with myself
[6] *Return to Paradise*, p.37

drawn to the highly personal music of his poems, won from the cast-iron mould of Afrikaans; a music twisted with the force of exorcism. Reading Breytenbach after leaving South Africa was like participating in a social and sensual act of linguistic revenge.

Raymond Carver was a survivor of North American working class deprivation, wrestling on the page against what he terms "the sense of doom and hopelessness".[7] He was also the survivor of four periods of hospitalization for acute alcoholism; he wrote during the last and most productive decade of his life in the intimate knowledge of death, and the discovery of new-found love.

Carver's prose characters, like the people he grew up amongst in the logging mills of Oregon and Washington, barely manage to find the words to say what they feel. They live in a vacuum of silence, sealed into a world of personal and material difficulty. It is this vacuum that Carver articulates in his prose, and breaks from in his poetry.

One tool he uses to great effect is a sort of muscular simplicity. "The words can be so precise they may even sound flat, but they can still carry; if used right, they can hit all the notes". [8] What better writer to happen upon at a time of mourning, when all verbal superfluity seemed to be an obstruction, when, as in Carver's poetry, life and death seemed like two lean blades sharpening each other, paring perception down to bare essentials.

In a very different context, Georges Perec was equally a survivor. He gives, as his deepest reason for writing, his parents' deaths in the Second World War, and the need to affirm his own life against their disappearance.[9] Capable of complex wordplay, in much of his prose he nonetheless uses language sparely, without self-indulgence, attempting to perceive as directly as possible the contours of the physical and human world around him; the same world whose destructive forces he had survived.

In *Je me souviens,* he is concerned with patterns of expression as impersonal as mathematical equations, as distant as the French formal mode of speech. As a result, the reader of *Je me souviens* might perceive, beyond the actual content of the book, the elusive rhythms and unpredictable paths of memory itself.

Lastly, there is the language of *Shooting at Sharpeville.* Ambrose Reeves was Bishop of Johannesburg until 1960. His

[7] Mona Simpson and Lewis Buzbee, "Raymond Carver", in Gentry and Stull (eds.), *Conversations with Raymond Carver*, p.33

[8] Carver, *Fires*, p.27

[9] *W ou le souvenir d'enfance*, p.64

book is intended as a direct act of political opposition, and as such deals head on, in clear, economical language, with the facts and strategies of oppression. What caught my attention as an adolescent, however, were not the words but the thirty black and white photographs sandwiched at the centre of the book. These photographs show the story of a massacre. The silence surrounding the photographs, filled with the latent roar of the events they record, drew me even closer to them. Could this possibly have happened so recently, and so close to home? They were to the blinded eye what words might be to a mute tongue.

WHITE SCARS

In writing this book, I found myself constantly needing to shift perspective, from the literary to the historical, from the linguistic to the intensely personal. I wanted to investigate four books but also plumb my own experience. I could do this best through brief segments of autobiography, as well as poems which, particularly when referring to South Africa, accelerated the journey into the past.

I decided to break the entire text into a series of fragments. What form would better reflect shifts in place and vision, deep uprooting and re-routing, the loss and gain of bonds, a switching of tongues? I do not imagine the present alignment of these fragments as definitive, and believe that they could also be fitted together quite differently:

> On my desk there is a stone with the word "Amen" on it,
> a triangular fragment of stone from a Jewish graveyard
>   destroyed
> many generations ago. The other fragments, hundreds
> upon hundreds,
> were scattered helter-skelter, and a great yearning,
> a longing without end, fills them all:
> first name in search of family name, date of death seeks
>   dead man's birthplace, son's name wishes to locate

[10] From "The Amen Stone" by Yehuda Amichai, *Open Closed Open*, p.1, tr. from the Hebrew by Chana Bloch and Chana Kronfeld

> name of father, date of birth seeks reunion with soul
> that wishes to rest in peace. And until they have found
> one another, they will not find perfect rest. [10]

I needed the gap between fragments, the imperfect fit, the unspoken thought and hidden cause, the unsealed entrance between uneven edges. Energy runs between these edges, released by the force that first cracked them apart.

This energy may go by many names: despair, obsession, necessity, desire. Derek Walcott, upon witnessing the dramatization of a Hindu epic in the village of Felicity, Trinidad, calls it love:

> Break a vase, and the love that reassembles the fragments is stronger than the love which took its symmetry for granted when it was whole. The glue that fits the pieces is the sealing of its original shape. It is such a love that reassembles our African and Asian fragments, the cracked heirlooms whose restoration shows its white scars. [11]

I felt that by using a fragmented form I could look at four books while at the same time piecing together something of my own cracked heirlooms, South African, European, Jewish, on the pages that follow.

---

[11] "Near Felicity, Listening to the Rain on a Statue's Forehead", in *The International Herald Tribune*, 10th December 1992, p.9. From Walcott's Nobel Prize acceptance speech.

PART ONE

Reminders for the Blind:

Shooting at Sharpeville
by Ambrose Reeves

THE INVISIBLE BACKGROUND

Shooting at Sharpeville is a book by Bishop Ambrose Reeves that has followed me across some 40 years of my life. When I was in my early teens, this book rendered visible to me an event which otherwise might have been reduced to little more than a name in a **litany***[1] of place-names summing up the violence of apartheid South Africa. And yet, until recently, I had barely read a word that was written in it.

Sharpeville is a black **township*** near Vereeniging, thirty miles south of Johannesburg where I once lived. But I did not know exactly where this township was, even after the massacre that occurred there in 1960. How many white South Africans, apart from members of the police force and army, train drivers and a scattering of those working in the social services, knew exactly where the townships were?

For the main part, with some notable exceptions, townships were set well away from the main road, and separated from the white city or town by a no man's land several miles wide. They were often contained by fences, within which they huddled, low, treeless, dull as dust. Had it not been for the static, noxious, sleet-grey pall of smoke that gathered over them from fires in winter, they might have been entirely camouflaged from the passing eye.

In fact, their names did not even appear on an ordinary road map. Their absence from such documents is one sign of the degree to which black, Indian and Coloured realities were illegible to white South Africans at that time.

21st MARCH, 1960

By the time I came to open *Shooting at Sharpeville*, I knew the same scant facts which were common knowledge in South Africa about what had happened there. A crowd had gathered at the police-station of a township to protest against the law which obliged all adult blacks in white urban areas to carry a "**pass***", an internal passport. The police had opened fire and killed sixty-nine people, most of them shot in the back while running away.

[1] Words marked with an asterisk are referred to in the WORDKEYS section appended to each of the four parts of this book.

I remember the grimness on the faces of my parents when they read the news of what had happened that day, and the flurry of emotion which followed. I was eight years old, and had never before seen a newspaper change the mood of adults in such a way. I remember, too, going with my father to visit some friends of his, Monty and Myrtle Berman, on the Sunday following the Sharpeville massacre. Somehow, I made a connection between the Sunday newspaper lying on the bedspread in their bedroom, and the fact that they were talking in such hushed, conspiratorial tones. I was told to go out and amuse myself in the garden.

Later that year, in the wake of the massacre and waves of protest around the country, a State of Emergency was declared. The Bermans were among the tens of hundreds of people arrested. The larger political parties acting in the name of the majority of people in the country were banned, and surviving groups were forced to rethink their strategies. The one to which my father belonged, the African Resistance Movement, turned to acts of sabotage, blowing up pylons of the kind that bear electric cables.

In July 1964, just before my thirteenth birthday, my father was arrested. After being detained in solitary confinement for three months he was only put on trial in November, together with several other members of the group. As a senior leader he received a nine-year sentence.

Empty as an ear

My father is in jail.
Where is my voice?
My voice is empty as an ear,
I cannot hear him.

My father is in jail.
What is there to say?
Words are for listening with,
I cannot hear him.

My father is in jail.
His silence fits my silence
like a glove.
I cannot hear my own voice,

the one I might finally
have torn loose from him,
had they not torn him
loose from me first

PATRIMONY

My father was the person I felt closest to in the world. His arrest marked me more strongly than any other event in my young adolescent life. At a time when many of my friends seemed to be glowing at the frontiers of sexual discovery, I withdrew deeply inside myself. And while some of them celebrated their bar mitzvahs, I, who had been discouraged from going through this ritual by my father, was faced with an unforeseen personal ritual of my own. On my thirteenth birthday, I left school early to pay him a visit. Perhaps because minors were not allowed into prison, the authorities decided this visit would take place outside The Fort in Johannesburg, where he was being held in solitary confinement. We sat talking at the back of a Volkswagen for the regulation half an hour, with two policemen sitting impassively in the front. The next time I saw him I was sixteen.

In the years of my father's absence, I was magnetically attracted to the objects he had left behind in our house. When I returned from school, I would hover around the desk where he had prepared his physics lectures and marked exam papers. I sifted through the objects in the drawers, among them pens, papers, his pipes and pipe cleaners. I removed his clothes from the plastic bags where they were stored in my parents' wardrobe, and sometimes tried them on. Above all, I went back, over and over, to his books.

There were books in almost all the rooms of our house, a multitude of them including novels, books on philosophy, history, science and art, filling shelves that in several rooms ran from floor to ceiling. It wasn't difficult to imagine that the walls of the house were themselves built of books. Most had my parents' first names written together on the flyleaf, almost forming a single name in my father's meticulous hand.

I spent untold hours examining their spines, blowing dust from their pages, opening and smelling them. I looted the juiciest amongst them, such as D.H. Lawrence's *Lady Chatterly's Lover.* But of all my parents' books, it was *Shooting at Sharpeville* that I returned to and pored over to the point of obsession.

For a while, on its arrival at our house in the early 1960's, this book remained in its lemon-yellow Victor Gollancz dust jacket, sharply bitten with crimson lettering. It was sub-titled "The Agony of South Africa", followed by a phrase in big black italics announcing a series of photographs and a foreword by Chief Albert Luthuli.

Some time before my father's arrest, *Shooting at Sharpeville* was banned. Since possession of it was now a criminal offence, it was placed on a bookshelf to the left of the fireplace in our living room, hidden from view behind a first row of books, wrapped in the suitably coloured dust jacket of Stendhal's *The Red and the Black.* Later, it found its way to a small bookshelf to the right of the door of my parents' bedroom, which was now occupied only by my mother.

IN MY PARENTS' ROOM

I enter my parents' room, still wearing the grey flannels and white shirt of my school uniform. If I have homework to do, I banish it from my mind. If my younger brother and sister are around, someone else is looking after them for the while.

The quietness of the house closes over me. The garden and the street could be asleep in broad daylight. There is not the ripple of another human presence.

I sit down cross-legged at the bookshelf and pull out Shooting at Sharpeville. *I already know the photographs at the centre of the book, but the knowledge does not lessen their mystery. There are thirty of them. They begin with an aerial photograph of the township of Sharpeville, the police station at its centre. This is the setting for the story they tell.*

Protesters cross the stubble field that surrounds the police station, and gather at the wire fence. It is a sunny day. Many of them wear hats, or doeks, some are in their shirtsleeves. There are a few parasols. Men and women raise their arms into the air, thumbs up.

Saracen tanks come rolling through the streets of the township. Blacks wave in greeting, a man at the tank hatch waves back. The police stand around a van and tank in the enclosure of the police station. Protesters press at the fence.

Police have mounted the turret of a tank and opened fire. Their indistinct firearms are circled in white.

The protesters take flight across the field: young women laughing in disbelief, a man pressing on the pedal of his bicycle as he mounts, two boys with outstretched arms intersecting in flight. There can be no greater need for movement with death at their backs, they must reach safety and yet the photograph arrests them where they run, they struggle not only against the speed of the bullets but also against the button of the camera that holds them still.

Next thing death has made its pick. The fallen lie in the stubble field, on the sand roads of the township, ungainly volumes of flesh with bullet holes in their backs, belly down in their own blood. Wounded survivors prop themselves up; one is given water by a priest.

Blacks look round, incredulous, numb, as police patrol the streets with sjamboks and rifles. Hats, shoes, jackets are scattered about them, then reappear heaped against the fence of the police station, the protest of the people of Sharpeville reduced to the debris of a disposable gravestone.

I return to the images of the dead, as if there were something that had escaped me, what can have escaped me in these images where no further escape is possible? Even the roads where they lie seem to go nowhere now.

Then, with a backward flip of the page I revive them, they are up and running, the living and the dead side by side.

I shut the book, and slide it into place on the shelf. The air is thick around me, dust motes in shafts of sunlight glitter like mica. I walk around aimlessly, down the corridor, into the kitchen for a drink, hemmed in by the walls of the house. Back in my parents' room I open the wardrobe, and remove some of my father's clothing from a plastic bag.

I sink my face into the softness of a woollen jersey, and breathe in what might be left of his smell. I feel the woven texture of a jacket, the smooth polished strip of a belt. Looking in the mirror, I try on one of his ties.

THE SILENT SOUNDTRACK

I was a secretive boy, and barely spoke to anyone about my father's arrest. By speaking I would have had to share something of my own painstakingly protected vulnerability, in some way confront those who chose not to acknowledge the arrest, speak of its connection with the world around us. Instead of breaking the silence in which I had already been accustomed to conducting my own affairs, my father's arrest drew me even further inwards.

The territory of my silence was invested not only with loss, but with a political meaning which left me feeling perplexed. I was proud of my father, what he had done must be politically right, yet politics had crossed the intimacy of our threshold to remove him, leaving behind a spoor of absence and pain. There was so much less space in the house now that he had gone. And the world outside the window was even further away.

Just as I found no way to speak of what was happening to me, I did not speak to anyone about the Sharpeville photographs. I knew, of course, that they were at the heart of a story, but I did not learn the full story. I read nothing of the text apart from the captions to the photographs.

The photographs themselves already revealed more than I could fully take in. They were part of another kind of secret, outside of my family, greater than anything I could find words for, joined somehow to the silence I kept concerning my father. They were always there waiting for me and I kept returning to them, as one returns to the crack in a door because there is something one must know yet fears to find out.

The more I did this, and the longer I did not speak about the photographs, the deeper the silence that accumulated around them, thick soundproof wads piling against the noise they were constantly on the verge of making.

There was the noise of the milling crowd, tanks rolling, men with mouths open and thumbs up. The noise of the crowd pressed against the police-station fence, and then the noise of running, the yelps and screams and cries, the crush of grass and whirr of bicycle wheels as bullets cracked the air. The low sobbing noise of those lying face down in the field or the road, voices of witnesses, executioners, survivors, boots and shoes on gravel. The serrated noise of ambulances arriving, followed by the mute half-circle of onlookers, with the grave thundering faces of those who have seen too much and can say too little.

When I closed the book they were still standing there in the last photograph, looking outwards, away from the two bodies lying before them, one covered in a pale blanket, the other in a leather jacket with arms clasped to one side. I put the book away, and the abysmal Sharpeville soundtrack went on twisting into the day; the wide, leafy, tranquil day beyond the window, filled with the whittled song of weaver birds, immaculately waxed cars breezing past the great plane trees, maids on the grass with legs straight out in front of them, shining cutlery till it sliced up the sunlight.

It was 1964 or 5 in the northern suburbs of Johannesburg, just a few years after Sharpeville, when rumour had it that the writing was on the wall for the whites; all this now apparently less than a memory. The worst thing that could hit the suburbs was a hailstorm. The warm air was perfumed with jasmine and amnesia on our **island*** of comfort, where the quietness could so easily be mistaken for peace.

Except that my father had been arrested in the course of a war. For years I had heard the low, smoky sound of his plotting in the company of visitors behind a shut door; had known that trouble was just around the corner, not much further away than our bugged telephone.

Out on the street beyond our plumbago hedge, you could witness it in other forms. The van planted discreetly on the tar, khaki members of the police-force rounding up black men who could not produce a pass, driving them off with their hands hooked into the stiff wire grill at the back like wind-blown leaves. Maids in pastel aprons and crimped caps, hotly gossiping out on the pavement, were momentarily turned to stone.

Or a white neighbour would hail a black man, an entire stranger to him, "Hey, **Jim***!", the words yellow as dog urine describing an arc of meaning: this is my place and you are not worth the weight of your own true human name here, Jim who is not Jim, as bad as another who is not Jim either, all of you nobody except in answer to my need.

There was a smouldering war on, but out in our streets all that could be seen of it were minute fragments of shrapnel flying from a mouth or an eye for half an instant before being buried in the slow, lazy pageant of days.

There was a war on: the Sharpeville photographs showed signs of recent battle, in which people who could easily have been the Jims and Reginas and Victorias of our kitchen sinks and rose beds punched a hole in the air and for a few mortal moments made their presence known.

Then their voices were snuffed out, while those other voices, in a guttural crush of command, made their loud equation of order and death. Afrikaans voices, since white policemen were most likely to be Afrikaans-speaking; old enemies of the English-speakers of the suburbs, yet doing their business in the name of all South African whites.

Marking time

The blacks lie dead.
Blood moves thick as roots
from their stomachs through the sand.

The blacks lie dead,
a road of them, a field of them,
they hold the world still with their gravity.

The living have nowhere to go,
neither policemen nor survivors
shift from their places,

all of them marking time.
Later, it will be said that this was history.
A red wind will pour through the trees

and March 1960 will belong to Sharpeville.
But for now history is a hidden photograph
that makes no sound,

history is a bullet hole
through which the dead
go **underground***.

"DEAD DAD..."

I won't say I feel angry or betrayed by my father after his arrest in 1964, but I cry myself dry behind my shut door and next afternoon run out onto the rugby field and pump the darkness from my body with every studded step of my boots, or jog till my breath rusts at the edges, heave oxygen back into myself but find no buoyancy.

When told I am lean as my mother I fail to believe it since a lean body would surely be lighter than mine. Anyway, I refuse all resemblance to my mother who is reeling with the effects of her own loss and does not receive me, I am my father's son, lamb of God, chosen one, look in the mirror and see his face in mine, think of him and my mind goes black as the mirror's back, a mourning band blindfolds my eyes.

I cannot admit I am in mourning since no one has died, but I do think the thought of being dead myself, over and over I push my wandering mind to the edge of oblivion and final effacement.

Next day I sit in the middle of the class with homework well done so that no teacher will notice me, and, preserving a gleam of presence in my glance while leaving the classroom almost entirely behind in my thoughts, still prepared to answer the next question about a square root or past participle, I practice the art of not being there, since there is no air there, no way of sharing the one and only absolute fact that concerns me: my father is gone.

Not once to any schoolmate or outside the walls of my family by blood or invention can I render his absence present in words, he is an unnamed space to them, a shame and a fear, off the map of what they can hear.

Worse.

He is a threat to my own invisibility.

He is something about me that everyone could see if they chose to, they might bury him under their silence and still know that he is there, doubly there in the silence that magnifies the dark ominous mystery around him, and wherever he is I am, while I want to be nowhere.

Comes the day when I cannot find him inside me, he is of course there but I no longer know where, closer than I want to know, something inside me has been arrested with him but I do not see this or say it, something inside me does not stop dying to be with him but I silence it to go on living.

What I do say, or rather write without realising it at the beginning of one regulation five hundred word letter, and only half believe when he tells me about it during the next half-hour visit, the actual words of betrayal are "Dead Dad", left there by the prison censor, in the mean lined and calculated space left for survival, blue on white at the top of the page for him to read.

At home I return to his debris. Crumbs of love. Relics of himself and the cause he gave himself to. My pride rises tall as a wall before the raw stretch of my sadness, since this is not simply loss, but loss in the name of the greater good.

I enter my parents' room, open the book. There are the living people of Sharpeville and the dead in whom defiance and ultimate consequence intersect, there I sit with my weight on the pine floorboards, watching the real, unspeakable world beyond the inward-facing one-way mirror of the Johannesburg suburbs.

"SHOOTING AT SHARPEVILLE"

Here is what a South African resident might have learnt about events at Sharpeville upon glancing at a newspaper on the morning after the massacre:

> At Sharpeville, Colonel Pienaar, in command of the police there, had to force his way through a crowd of about 20, 000 Bantu who had surrounded the police station [...] Stones rained on the police and the mob advanced on them. Colonel Pienaar then gave orders for the police to load. At that moment three shots were fired at the police from within the Bantu crowd. The shouting crowd advanced and the police fired a volley with Sten guns and .303's without an order having been given to fire.[2]

These are not the words of a journalist, but of Prime Minister Verwoerd, addressing the House of Assembly. Although he mentions that the facts have not been checked, his statement reads like an unconditional affirmation.

It was in the face of this version of events, and in order to ascertain the truth of what happened, that Ambrose Reeves wrote *Shooting at Sharpeville.* The photographs included in his book disprove several elements of Verwoerd's statement; so does the evidence he records, some of it brought before the government's own Commission of Enquiry. What emerges from the book is not simply an account of events at Sharpeville, but a biopsy of South Africa as it entered the violent political silence of the 1960's.

Unable to take in Reeves' account as a teenager, I have only recently read it for the first time, in an attempt to understand what lay behind the photographs that held such fascination for me. *Shooting at Sharpeville* seems to have lost nothing of its immediacy in the interim.

Reeves tells the story of the massacre with tight, dispassionate economy. He departs from his factual, urgent account only when referring to his own religious convictions, and even then makes it clear that he believes South Africa is nearing an unnamed disaster. The police force, he claims, has taken on "the functions

2 "Verwoerd Gives Riot Details", *Cape Times*, 22nd March 1960

of an army of occupation"[3], the implication being that the country is at war.

Reeves begins by describing black communities in various parts of South Africa in the 1950's, their daily lives edged with threat and deprivation, particularly if they did not bend to the demand of servility. Yet these same communities offered resistance to government policy in general, and the pass laws in particular. They did so not only out of political conviction but also a tenacious sense of pride and tradition. One such community, many of its members belonging to the Bafurutse tribe, lived in the township of Sharpeville, just outside of Vereeniging.

According to Reeves, the crowd which gathered around the fence of the police-station at Sharpeville on 21st March 1960 to protest against the pass laws was not more than 5,000 strong.

Some members of this crowd were activists of the Pan Africanist Congress, which was running a campaign to resist the pass laws, but others were simply local residents. A few had been bullied or at least strongly encouraged to be present, and at least one bus-driver was pursued when he tried to leave, according to an eye-witness account at the Commission of Enquiry into the massacre.[4] But the majority assembled of their own free will.

It was a Monday morning. The bus service had been halted, preventing people from going to work. They came to get some idea of what was going on, to watch the aeroplanes circling overhead, or the Saracen tanks which some had never seen before. It was rumoured that the Bantu Commissioner was on his way to address them, and they were intrigued: "We have trouble with regard to the passes, and we just want to hear; to hear what the Europeans have to say about it".[5] They bore no weapons, apart from a few sticks and pieces of iron. Some shouted slogans; others sang hymns, such as "Abide with Me".

The police, it seems, panicked. Their newly arrived commander, Lieutenant-Colonel Pienaar, was ill-informed. He did not know how many men he had under his command, or what armaments they disposed of. Neither he, nor any other policeman, tried to make meaningful contact with the crowd. Reeves suggests that, in the absence of the humility and unquestioning deference which they generally expected, they imagined themselves to be

---

3 *Shooting at Sharpeville*, p.21

4 pp.127-141

5 p.135

confronted with an atmosphere of riot and rebellion. As Pienaar put it before the Commission: "The Native mentality does not allow them to gather for a peaceful demonstration. For them to gather means violence."[6]

If this was what the Lieutenant-Colonel thought, then he would not have been able to even conceive of a crowd of black people that had gathered to see, to listen and perhaps to speak. He was faced with a reality so unlikely that it had to be obliterated with bullets. He accordingly lined up his men like "a firing squad".[7]

In the space of 40 blind seconds, without any warning whatsoever, they had fired off 700 rounds, killing 69 people including 8 women and 10 children, wounding 180 (31 women and 19 children). Seventy per cent of these people were shot in the back while running away. But some were not even at the police-station fence. Several were passing by in nearby streets, one was in a shop. Another was on his lawn reading a book.

"The way of apartheid", Reeves concludes, "is a way of death and not of life".[8] He points out not only how the events at Sharpeville, and elsewhere, ripped into the lives of the black population, but also how the system was "beginning to sap the vitality and blunt the moral sense of some of the white people."[9] One chilling example of this came from Lieutenant-Colonel Pienaar himself, when asked at the Commission of Enquiry if he had learned any useful lesson from the massacre: "Well we may get better equipment", he replied.[10]

Reeves expresses the intuition that the time of peaceful protest was over in South Africa. Two years later, Nelson Mandela intimated at his trial that revolt might be the only response left to his people. But even before that, in the days and weeks following the Sharpeville massacre, the apparent tranquillity of the country was shaken by a period of violent confrontation.

WAKE

On 21st March 1960, the day of the Sharpeville massacre, there were also protests against the pass laws in the townships of Langa

---

[6] *Shooting at Sharpeville*, p.95
[7] p. 91
[8] p. 105
[9] p. 96
[10] p. 93

and Nyanga, outside Cape Town. That same night a crowd attacked policemen, stormed and set fire to municipal offices, severed telephone wires and set up road-blocks to keep fire engines out. There followed a violently repressed two-week strike, during which Philip Kgosana of the Pan Africanist Congress led a protest march of 30,000 people through Cape Town.[11] Two days earlier, on 28th March, a successful national one-day stay-away strike was called by Chief Albert Luthuli, President of the African National Congress. 10,000 people marched through Durban.

The government was galvanised into cold repression, beginning with the imposition of a five-month State of Emergency. As investors shifted capital out of South Africa, more than 1,900 activists were arrested, while the African National Congress and the Pan Africanist Congress were outlawed under the Suppression of Communism Act.

Shooting at Sharpeville was among those books banned at the time. Its author, Anglican Bishop of Johannesburg and a British national, doggedly opposed to apartheid policy, was deported. Both the concrete evidence of what had actually happened on 21st March 1960, and a man who had defiantly recorded that evidence, were removed from the public eye.

21st MARCH 1968

In South Africa, the name "Sharpeville" came to signify far more than a massacre, more than the violence that could be unleashed in the name of apartheid. It signalled a terrible promise for some, an unthinkable threat for others, the mortal price of a disputed order which had not yet been fully paid, a time-bomb that went on silently ticking.

Sharpeville, at least for a short while, lay at the root of a graph of panic rising behind a white facade of certainty; *sharp ville*, an invisible city whose whirring blades of retribution might spin loose any moment, fanning chaos before it while blood soaked into the streets behind, raising old ghosts of war across the country.

Sharpeville soon became a memory that the state wanted buried by means of censorship and other instruments of silence.

---

11 Pampallis, *Foundations of the New South Africa*, p.211

This did not prevent Mafika Gwala from writing: "I'm one of the surviving children of Sharpeville/ Whose black mothers spelled it out in blood".[12]

Most whites chose to shut their ears, though for those who chose to listen, the massacre went on speaking from underground. Ingrid de Kok in her poem "My Sharpeville" remembers "the dead, buried in voices that reached even to my gate".[13]

As a student at the University of the Witwatersrand, Johannesburg, I was amongst those who witnessed what happened when this memory was hung out in the open for all to see.

During my first year of study I was a member of The Human Rights Society on campus, chaired at the time by Ian Margo. Following a suggestion by Neville Colman, we decided to commemorate the eighth anniversary of the Sharpeville massacre by exhibiting large-format prints of the photographs that appeared in Ambrose Reeves' book, in the upstairs foyer of the Student Union Building.

We also stretched a big banner which read "REMEMBER SHARPEVILLE" between two poles facing the grey Romanesque eyesore of the university's administrative and teaching hub, the Central Block. No one could miss it. The cocky, muscular, sharp-tongued mob that had gathered there by mid-morning soon built up the steam to tear it down, and stamp on its plastic skin until small stones stuck through.

The collective blood was up now and with a hungering din the mob advanced along the tar path which divided the campus down the middle, Mining Geology block left and Social Sciences right, students of commerce and engineering and dentistry shoulder to shoulder and crotch against neck.

With slow, jovial urgency, bloated with bad language, they advanced to the swimming pool at the end of the path, turning right to the plate-glass windows of the Student Union Building. The door had been hastily locked and they threatened to burst it inwards, whipping themselves up into a frenzy with catcalls and rugby chants.

At the same time, a rumour spread that the police were on their way. There was a brief moment of hesitation amongst those of us who were inside the building, after which the photographs were

---

12 "Getting off the Ride", *Jol'iinkomo*, p.63

13 *Familiar Ground*, p.13

unpinned from their black panels. The din of the mob dropped to the low rumble of animals at feeding time.

Then everyone went back to lectures as usual. Now that the banner and photos were down, perhaps members of the mob believed that an irksome memory had been obliterated. What had happened eight years earlier could after all hardly be said to have happened. Had the spool of time not been miraculously rewound, the voices of Sharpeville returned to humble breasts, the first of seven hundred rounds of bullets still lying cold in the breech of invisible firearms?

But the silence on the campus, and in the streets outside, was not quite the same now. History had been glimpsed, not just in a book but in a public place, like a stranger who had been banished beyond the city walls but managed to slip in secretly. For just a moment, history was there for anyone to see, the faces and fists and crushed grass and guns, lined up and waiting at the blind limit of our lives.

Litany

"A series of petitions for use in church services or processions", or "a tedious recital", as in "a litany of woes" (Concise Oxford Dictionary).

Politically, a litany may be an inventory spoken to fuel a complaint, protest or celebration, stringing together a rosary of well-known items in ritual fashion. Listeners might respond as they would in church to the call of the clergy.

In apartheid South Africa, litanies of victims, and/or heroes, or key places, were gathered together on both sides of the ideological divide, as if the largest collection of names might occupy a wider moral territory for its collective owner. While schoolchildren recited lists of battlefields and Great Trek leaders, all of them grist for the National Party mill, poets such as Ingrid Jonker and Adam Small offered a very different litany, reminding the reader of state violence and deprivation:

> The child is not dead
> not at Langa not at Nyanga
> not at Orlando not at Sharpeville
> not at the police station in Philippi
> where he lies with a bullet through his brain.[14]

and

> ja in Bethlehem Lord
> in the stable
> by the donkey
> by the cow
> in the crib
> on the earth floor
> on the floor of sand Lord
> in a place that stank
> in a place where a person got sick from the stink

---

14 Ingrid Jonker, "The Child Who Was Shot Dead by Soldiers in Nyanga", tr. from the Afrikaans by Jack Cope and William Plomer, in *Selected Poems,* p.27.

we know such places Lord
ja we know them
we got duplicates of them allover
in Windemere
in Distrik Six
in Blouvlei here jis otherside Wynberg by Retreat[15]

The poet selects places as part of an incantation of memory, in a climate of official refusal to accept that there might be a history and a geography which is not white. As the places are set side by side, in turn recalling still other unnamed places, an alternative symbolic map is created, its surface torn with wounds that might otherwise have been wrapped in oblivion. This act of memory, which is also an act of resistance, becomes one of the functions of the poet, just as a traditional African poet might be called upon to remember the exact site of a well in the desert.[16]

As the history of South Africa changes, so do the litanies. The lament or reminder of the asphyxiating 60's (Jonker, Small), becomes a call, gathering with the dizzy momentum of the 90's. Those who have witnessed the wake of destruction in place after place, are now joined in a widening blood bond. War has given them "a history to wear", as in the poem by Karen Press, "Tiresias in the City of Heroes":

'Are you not bigger than your own backyard?
In that war each of us became the nation:
the whole nation entered into each of us.
Tell us that story.'

That story. That story:
In Sharpeville your arms died.
In Uitenhage your tongues died.
In Boipatong your eyes died.
In Katlehong and Bekkersdal and Empangeni
you died and you died and you died.
That's what I remember.

And then:

---

[15] Adam Small, "Great Krismis Prayer", tr. from the Afrikaans by Mike Dickman, in Hirson (ed.), *The Lava of this Land*, p.30

[16] Antjie Krog, *The Country of my Skull*, p.222

> In Pretoria your fingernails became joint chief of staff.
> In Pretoria your teeth ran the central bank.
> In Pretoria your hair was the president.
> That's what I remember.[17]

Even the capital is joined into the litany of blood, as torn body parts are visited upon those who occupy the seat of power. There is a sort of terrible transplant surgery going on throughout the nation, a sewing together of the body politic. But still no rest is to be found in a landscape where every surface has been stripped raw:

> My home is a place I'm frightened of. It's a big sore inside me that burns when I touch it.[18]

Location, Township

As early as 1820, British Settlers were "located" in buffer zones known as "locations" from which they were not allowed to move, in order to keep black tribes at bay.[19] By 1929, "township" was used to designate a restricted place of black (later also Coloured or Indian) habitation. Under apartheid, the two names became synonymous.

A "location" was not a neutral geographical position, but historically a place where residents were ordered to stay put: a town ship, cut loose from the moorings of the white city, the shores of money and political power. Residents, particularly when black, were cornered as a labour force; they were, in effect, living in "warehousing for migrant labour".[20] They returned from the white city at night, after hours jammed in buses, trains, and (as of the 1980's) mini-bus taxis, potentially primed with the implosive energies of humiliation, in turn vented against the closest available victims, often women or children.

And should these energies ever be expressed outwardly, the boundaries of townships (or locations) were carefully sealed off, riot control being one element taken into account in their conception:

---

[17] *Home*, p. 66

[18] as above

[19] *A Dictionary of South African English*, p.425

[20] Lindsay Bremner, "Crime and the Emerging Landscape of Post-Apartheid Johannesburg", in Hilton and Vladislavic (eds.), *Architecture, Apartheid and After* , p. 55

> The width of the roadways would have to be sufficient to allow a Saracen[tank] to execute a U-turn[...] the distance between houses had to be kept above a given minimum, and the houses had to be aligned so that firing between houses would not be impeded, and so that there would be no shelter for a fugitive. The distance between the boundaries of a township and the main highway had to be beyond the range of a .3O3 rifle.[21]

"Location" and "township", like those other terms of apartheid designating places where the lives of blacks were regimented to suit white needs, such as the "Bantustan" or sweetly cynical "homeland", the "resettlement area" and "closer-settlement camp", all referred to politically frozen zones; amputated portions of the country laid down in the dust of no man's land.

Yet it was the blacks who travelled across this no man's land most often, filling jobs for whites in their towns and cities by day, and draining out at night; blacks not whites who, despite the legal restrictions placed on their movements, crossed constantly between the walled fragments of South African space:

> The Golden City belongs to the white people of South Africa, and the Dark City to the black people. The Saturdays and Sundays of Alexandra roar, groan and rumble, like a troubled stomach. The same days in Johannesburg are as silent as the stomach of a dead person. The weekdays of Alexandra are those of a place which has been erased; in Johannesburg, week days are like a time when thousands of people arrive in a place at the end of a pilgrimage [...][22]

Alexandra was one of the few, older townships directly adjoining a white town or city, in this case just north of Johannesburg. In his poem "Alexandra", Wally Serote finds in this place a strong, mothering power:

---

[21] Baruch Hirson, *Year of Fire, Year of Ash*, p. 184, citing an interview with Professor Alan Lipman

[22] Wally Serote, *To Every Birth its Blood*, p.28

[...] we have only one mother, none can replace,
Just as we have no choice to be born,
We can't choose mothers;
We fall out of them like we fall out of life to death.

And Alexandra,
My beginning was knotted to you,
Just like you knot my destiny.
You throb in my inside silences
You are silent in my heart-beat that's loud to me.
Alexandra often I've cried.
When I was thirsty my tongue tasted dust,
Dust burdening your nipples.[23]

Alexandra – from the Greek "helper and defender of mankind" - was named after Queen Alexandra, wife of Edward VII. Proclaimed a white working-class suburb in 1905, it failed to attract white buyers and was settled by blacks as of 1912.[24] So, as in Serote's poem, a white colonial queen loses her identity to a local black mother.

I imagine apartheid Johannesburg as a gawky, golden eyed adolescent with hands unopened like flower bulbs, firmly tucked in a blanket to the back of a black township named Alexandra.

Suspended above the ground, feet dangling loose, he is lulled into an endless dream by her movements, oblivious to the bounds of her life, her cramped living quarters, feudal small change, scattered family. He is barely conscious of her presence though she is constantly before and below him, her heat and the smell of her hair, cheap skin cream and starched work-clothes, entering his body and his breath. She is someone else's mother, and it is more than anything else her motherhood he breathes in, not seeing the absence of her child but held in her mothering arc in the place of that child. She goes about her daily duties, polishing the stoep, slicing paw-paw, airing the beds, serving his space having deserted her own.

The years pass and she ages, while he remains an adolescent strapped to her back. Only those whose feet touch the ground can truly grow upward. Nor can she turn him out of the house: she is not his mother, and this is not her place, which lies just outside

23 *Yakhal'inkomo*, p.30

24 Lindsay Bremner, "Crime and the Emerging Landscape of Post-Apartheid Johannesburg", in Judin and Vladislavic (eds.), *Architecture, Apartheid and After*, p.50

the city, on the main road leading north into the heart of Africa. She bears him piggy-back across the apartheid years. It might take him a lifetime to find his feet.

Pass

It sat in the pocket of a black man and later also a black woman, a document which by the early 1960's ran to 96 pages, recording the holder's name, place of origin, tribal affiliation and chief, place and date of birth, father's birth-place. It also gave a history of previous employment, told whether taxes had been paid. Crucially, it included pages for a current employer's regular dated signature to prove the holder was working. It was indispensable in order to get a job, find housing, or get married. Anyone caught without an up to date pass risked being arrested, jailed, mistreated, and "endorsed out" of white urban territory, where only sufficient black workers were tolerated to satisfy white needs.

Ambrose Reeves points out that in the year 1957 alone, three years before the Sharpeville massacre, "365,000 Africans were convicted of one offence or another against the pass laws"; this amounts to 1,000 offences per day.[25]

Historically, its use was recorded in South Africa from the eighteenth century onwards, tracing territorial limits for various groups including "all strangers travelling beyond the Kloofs" (1806); "all slaves cutting wood for fuel" (1812); British settlers of 1820 wishing to "leave their allotted holdings at Bathurst".[26]

At the time of apartheid, when whites were not required to carry any identity papers, it was variously known or named as a pass book, reference book, book of life, passport to existence, dog licence.

It spawned other words describing various forms of administrative enforcement and resistance: pass-law, pass system, pass offence and offender, pass office, pass raid, pass arrest, pass-burner.

Out in the suburbs of the white city, once again I see the police get out of their van, stop a man and ask for his pass. At the side of

---

[25] *Shooting at Sharpeville*, p.29

[26] *A Dictionary of South African English*, citing various sources, p.543

the road, where hoopoes nest in a gap near the bottom of a stone wall and foliage softly brushes over the top. The police wait as the man puts his hand in his breast pocket to produce the document, and in that split second the barbed fences of an administrative camp push up through the warm lazy tar to surround him, a maze of restrictions binding his body as the air is drawn taut, the light breeze anaesthetized.

The man is so apparently compliant, impassive. He might just as well be laid out in the efficient quietness of an operating theatre, under the surgeon's knife. During the operation, he loses his tongue.

Composer Todd Matshikiza describes a night raid:

> They fling their young rugby playing bodies in my direction and say the familiar password, 'Ja, jong, Ja,' which means 'Declare your damned self, Jong.' How does one declare oneself out of a withered, crumpled, shapeless near-discoloured overcoat; out of a sleepless bundle of a jumpy mass, frightened of your papers which are several and none of them in order [...]. They came bouncing towards me. "Speak fast, jong, haven't you got a blerry tongue? Where's your pass?"[27]

The pass, also known as a "dompas", dumb pass. Dumb as in stupid, but also dumb as in voiceless, since the pass-holder's political voice had been sequestered. The pass was the stamp of the administration upon a politically mute and estranged life.

Pylon

I knew, after my father's trial, that he had been involved in the blowing up of pylons. What I did not know was that blowing up pylons was already quite a game in South Africa before people such as my father came onto the scene. In 1942, a group of extreme right-wing Afrikaners chose this way of disrupting the gold-mines, showing how much they disapproved of General Smuts' British sympathies.[28] Future Prime Minister D.F.Malan's parliamentary

[27] *Chocolates for my Wife*, p.126

[28] Eric Walker, *A History of Southern Africa,* p.717

statements were an invitation to sabotage: republican secession, according to him, was preferable to Commonwealth membership; the Japanese were "blameless", and "the Germans were bound to win the war".[29]

In our high school history book, Malan was presented as a benevolent founding father, a bastion of order. Against his ilk, I held the secret of my own father. I imagined him driving our car off into the heart of the night, planting sticks of dynamite at the foot of a pylon, and driving back with the wind in his face as great wheels of flame and dust rolled into the blackness behind him.

After his imprisonment, I thought of him when I passed the lines of giant headless pylons bearing their cables across the wasteland at the outskirts of Johannesburg. He must have driven along that same road, sizing them up and plotting their downfall.

At high school, our class was presented with an English poem by Cecil Day-Lewis, chanting the praise of pylons which brought progress across hill and dale. What was I to do with this? In my father's terms, it was the *bringing down* of pylons that was supposed to open the gateway to progress.

Pylons were a puzzle to me, a source of light and power, a source of darkness in my mind, a reminder of the bomb blasts that had buckled some of their number while the rest just went on motionlessly marching. Had my father's activities changed anything in South Africa? The pylons still crossed the land, and he was gone.

Although he writes (with not a little self-searching) about sabotage in his autobiography, mentioning dynamite, timing devices and detonators, there is no description of what he actually did.[30] In fact he organised, but was not personally involved in, the blowing up of pylons.

Until recently, I had only the vaguest idea of what blowing up a pylon might concretely entail. But then Hugh Lewin, who was given a seven-year sentence in the same trial as my father, and served it in the same prison, sent me a poem he had written in 1970, "Pylon". Here is the act of planting dynamite spelled out in kinetic detail:

---

[29] as above

[30] Baruch Hirson, *Revolutions in my Life*, pp. 298–324

It's too late now
to stop, so go in
bowed, silent
beneath the wires and arching beams
where the throbbing is all around
in the ground
in the sky.

Go in with your packages,
mean gifts for a king.

Hurry now - and careful.
Bind them tight. Right - tight
And for God's sake don't plug in till the circuit's fixed
Right - and check your packet - right, right.
Now the timer
  ticking, ticking
  loud, even with the hum.

  Big bastard, isn't he?

And now, set? Set.
If there's anything wrong here
this'll blast us with it. Set
and now, carefully, plug
in.

O.K.

Above the throbbing and the hum
you can feel the quiet ticking
and grass seeds begin to itch.

Let's go.

Tomorrow morning, big boy, you'll blow.[31]

When I first read this, I had the dizzy sensation of being whipped back into the thick of an old half-obscured dream filled with flame and dust whirling in slow motion, airborne girders and wires and debris floating and twirling and flickering in the half-

[31] *Bandiet out of Jail,* p.204 (poem in slightly different form here)

light of destruction and hope; a dream that went on detonating inside me while my father was confined in the silence of a place beyond reach.

A text can itself be fixed with a timing device which goes off at some unforeseeable time in the future.

Island

Our house in Johannesburg was an island, the front door marked with an invisible cross, since the man who once lived there had betrayed the moral precepts and material ease of the white community in the name of an alien vision. Would his family not be prepared to do the same? No act of aggression was perpetrated against the house. Instead, a sea of silence was raised against it. We were unnamed castaways. Almost no one in the neighbourhood spoke a word of my father's imprisonment, nor did we speak to them of it. But many knew, and they knew that we knew that they knew, and our silence was sealed within their silence.

At the same time, white English-speaking Johannesburg was itself an island, with its treasure of gold, ringed by the dry wastes of a no man's land, and beyond that the labour pool of the townships. Not many Afrikaners could find a place for themselves in a city whose land had once been part of a Boer Republic, conquered during the Boer War (Why not "the British War", given British greed for diamonds and gold?)

Johannesburg: a golden magnet, with no natural source of water to soften its abrupt presence at the end of the nineteenth century, attracted to itself a bustling, hard-eyed, sharp-witted, covetous field of energy. At the edge of this field, there welled a latent tide of retribution:

> Now the siren wails over houses crouching
> behind flowery hedges where the roads fork.
> Doors of courthouses slam shut, the veil
> of the temple of money tears.
> In lecture halls the lights go out. In warm
> shafts the water surges, glistening, flows
> rippling over the gold-warted city.[32]

[32] from "Housebreaking of the Mamba", by Wilma Stockenström, 1970, tr. from the Afrikaans by Johann de Lange, in Hirson (ed.), *The Lava of this Land*, p.105

I come from an island within an island, which lies within another island, South Africa, severed from the continent, surrounded on three sides by ocean, and on the fourth by desert (Namibia), sparsely populated farmland (Botswana, Zimbabwe), the Limpopo River, and dense subtropical vegetation (Mozambique).

To these natural barriers, white settlers added their own multitude of thorny hedges, walls and electrified fences, cleaving the country from its continent till it might just as well have been called "South of Africa".

But when people in South Africa spoke quietly about "The Island", they were referring to a fourth island, off the Cape coast, Robben Island, where South Africa's black male political prisoners were held. Since Mandela and others returned to the main(is)land in the 1990's, the country has begun its drift back to the continent, while in swelling numbers its poor, and those of many other African countries, come pressing against the bulwarks of its inner island-cities.

Jim

There was also "John", and "Jack", as well as "Chief", but in Johannesburg, as far as I remember, the first forename that came into a white's mind when addressing a black man was "Jim". " 'What's your name, Jim?' he asked. 'Johannes, Baas,' the man said".[33] "Jim comes to Joburg" was the catch-all title given to any number of stories about greenhorn migrants arriving in the big city.

Why Jim? Perhaps this name was simply one of the briefest ways of designating someone, a first name only, as if the person were a child, so that his adulthood and singular identity could be negated at the same time. Who knows what associations sharpened the blade of a name such as Jim, only one banal word among many in the artillery of daily contempt, but a key one because it designated a potentially potent enemy.

I have an Afrikaans-English dictionary[34] which lists the word "Jim" in the English section. One of the translations of this name into Afrikaans is given as "Jim Crow, (Amerikaanse Neger)". Jim

[33] D. Bee, *Children of Yesterday*, quoted in *A Dictionary of South African English*, p.331

[34] Bosman, van der Merwe and Hiemstra, Tweetalige Woordeboek, first ed. 1931, seventh ed. 1967

Crow was the name of a negatively portrayed black character in a popular North American nineteenth century minstrel show.

The next entry in the same dictionary is "jimjams", the jitters, delirium tremens.

Whatever lies behind the name Jim, any number of respectable white ladies and gentlemen chose to use it. Some did this with a tone of apparently light indifference. Some expelled the name forcibly from the gut and out through the teeth before going on to issue an order. As if the other, unacknowledged, not truly named and therefore not fully contained, had entered an unbearable zone of proximity. As if there were a need to evacuate the other's presence from inside oneself. As if the other were a foreign body.

"Jim", from "James", whose original Hebrew meaning is "the supplanter".

The white mouth spat, the black mouth swallowed back, all in the space of seconds, in the sunlight and the smell of gardens and the guise of peace. But the name had entered the black man's body, and would not lie still:

> It starts
> as a murmur
> from one mouth to another
> in a rhythm of ribaldry
> that rises to a crescendo
> Abelungu ngo'dam – Whites are damned
> Basibiza ngo Jim – they call us Jim.[35]

Underground

Certain elements moving underground in the Johannesburg area before or around the time of the Sharpeville massacre:

Rain water, driving in a steep mud-red rush down the gutters of our road, some of it gulped by storm water drains with a deep, hoarse noise above a distant drone as if the whole slope were inwardly roaring while excess water bloated on, bearing its wild promise to the bottom of the hill and the black iron railing of the zoo.

---

[35] Oswald Mtshali, "A Roadgang's Cry", *Sounds of a Cowhide Drum*, p.13

Pipes and wires shifting tame water, electricity, waste. Black men lifted picks in unison and sang in captured virile voices, breaking into old tar with a rhythmic blunt clang to lay these channels down.

Human residents. Dugmore Boetie's adopted "father" schooled him "on the numerous small tunnels that start in and around Sophiatown [...] I was taught when and how to take advantage of them [...] where they led to, and what to do in case of rain. It was like a game of snakes and ladders with the ladders crossed out [...] The snakes swallowed us, and when we crawled out of their bowels we found ourselves back in our underground home [...] arms heavily laden with stolen goods."[36]

Miners. They shored up cyanide-bitten, burnt yellow dumps of waste against the south side of the city, and dust from there blew the homes of the gentry northward. Cumbersome iron mine-heads broke the skyline beyond Johannesburg, blue-gums used for props added their lanky form and spiced sickle leaves to road-sides, the whole city raised up the rump of its soul for gold. But no one saw the miners. They were gone miles down squeezing through tunnels, a core of light fixed at their brows and fingers of dynamite in their hands, bodies jittery with drill bits as they pierced galleries of permanent night.

My father. Just going out for a walk, he said after dinner, in the State of Emergency months after the Massacre, but often he didn't come back: "... took part in family activities, read to Denis and Allen, had supper, and then left for the night".[37] Underground. I imagined him walking between fences and foliage and the dry crackling fire of dog barks till the tar of the road opened up and he went down; to either side of him a shale face, the tunnelling of worms and rodents, dassies, glittery weave of ants and termites. There would be others in deep discussion, plotting, moving across earth and moonlight, "at night we typed the copy [of the clandestine broadsheet 'Spark'] on stencils while someone kept guard",[38] stoking the fire of their delayed dreams.

[36] Dugmore Boetie, *Familiarity is the Kingdom of the Lost*, p.10

[37] Baruch Hirson, *Revolutions in my Life*, p.296

[38] as above

Underground. Flying ants, emerging after a heavy fall of rain when the crust of ground softened: an endless whorl of them, glass wing slivers glittering from under a mound of weed into the sun's low beam, drifting in all directions to storm the windows of houses where electric lights hung like forbidden luminous fruit.

PART TWO

W/rites of Passage:

Die Ysterkoei Moet Sweet
(The Iron Cow Must Sweat)
by Breyten Breytenbach

DAUGHTER, PUMPKIN, MOON

Some time in 1972 a friend of mine, Robert Berold, came to visit me at our house in Johannesburg. He had just found a short story in Afrikaans that he was excited about. He read it out to me. My Afrikaans was terrible, but he didn't know this. I caught a few words glimmering at the surface of the text, amongst them "daughter", "pumpkin", "moon". Much was in darkness. Robert, however, was bubbling over with enthusiasm. Jung, he said. The unconscious. The power of the images. What I answered I can't remember, but he seemed to think we were in agreement. So why didn't we translate the story into English? Or rather, since it was poetry we were both interested in, and since the story was by the poet Breyten Breytenbach, why didn't we translate some of his poems into English? O.K., I replied in the heat of the moment, let's.

Not long afterwards I went to the main library at the University of the Witwatersrand and, for the first time in my life, willingly took out a book in Afrikaans. It was Breytenbach's first collection of poetry, a hard-covered copy of *Die Ysterkoei Moet Sweet* (The Iron Cow Must Sweat). I opened it, looked inside it, sat down cross-legged on the floor and went on looking while a horribly familiar feeling came over me, a mixture of incomprehension and deep, barely acknowledged recoil. I closed the book and put it back on the shelf.

But just a few years later, an entirely unpredictable circumstance led me to open another copy of *Die Ysterkoei Moet Sweet*, and wrestle with the contents till its spine was bent inward. I was no longer in the one country in the world where Afrikaans is widely spoken; apparently, however, my relationship with this language was not yet over.

IN AN ARK ON A HILLTOP AFTER THE FLOOD OF EMPIRE

Most English-speaking whites in the comfortable northern suburbs of Johannesburg at the time of apartheid, lived at an unquestioned remove from various other South African languages.

All around us were blacks speaking African languages: Ndebele, Sesotho, Sesotho sa Leboa, Setswana, Swati, Tshivenda, Xhosa, Xitsonga and Zulu. Today, together with English and Afrikaans, these constitute South Africa's eleven official languages. To white ears they often were – and still are – noise.

This noise, servant noise, rose up in the backyard of the home, in the kitchen, on the phone, on Radio Bantu, in the street, at the bus-stop, in exclamations and sentences and songs, part of the background against which white suburban life was lived. When whites and blacks spoke to each other, it was usually in various versions of the language that reigned there, which, again in the northern suburbs of Johannesburg, was English. The blacks did not always master this language, but were mastered by it; whites abused it by baby-talking down to them.

In officially bilingual South Africa, the tongue of power was forked: English for cash and Empire, Afrikaans for the cosh of political control after the National Party won the white elections of 1948.

These two languages were considered by their speakers to be entirely separate from each other, governed by a sense of hermetic **purity***. Any suggestion that Afrikaans might be infiltrated by elements of other languages would generally have been considered heretic. South African English, too, was considered to be as clean as the Queen's tongue. In reality, each was spiked with words and expressions from the other, as well as from black languages, Khoi-San, Malayo-Javanese and more. Not only vocabulary but syntax itself was altered as languages left their print on each other. At the same time, for long-standing political and social reasons, whites speaking one of the two "white" languages often saw speakers of the other as unwelcome invaders.

Afrikaans came to the northern suburbs of Johannesburg in a number of guises. It came with the police on their pass raids; the postman and his leather pouch aiming imperatives at the black assistant lumbering behind with a canvas sack; likewise, with assorted drivers and foremen and masters and **baase*** lording it over road-gangs and workers in baggy overalls.

Afrikaans, in this context, was the language of white working class people who controlled those even further down in the dust below them, in the name of the security and comfort of mainly

English-speaking whites. It was a bully-tongue of instruction and order, delivered briefly, bluntly and unbeautifully.

There was also the Afrikaans of the law makers, which we heard in snatches on the wireless. This was a language as remote as a celestial megaphone. From a discreet, indecipherable distance its Germanic martial rhythm was intended to hold sway over all of life around us.

To schoolchildren, Afrikaans was the language in which the national **anthem*** sometimes had to be sung, hundreds of mechanical throats delivering it every so often at school assembly. And then there was the compulsory Afrikaans class, which for me filled with an increasingly impenetrable fog, year after unavoidable year.

After high-school, many boys entered the army, myself among them. There, our knowledge of Afrikaans was enriched, particularly as concerns that portion of anatomy between the hips and the thighs, front and even more frequently back, so intimately bound up with obedience and the business of imposing it. This meant depositing upon the heads of those below what those above had in turn had noisily deposited upon them.

All in all, Afrikaans was not exactly cause for jubilation. As for Afrikaans speakers, they were the butt of bawdy jokes which depicted them somewhere on the scale of evolution between the warthog and the tank. "Afrikaner vrot banana!" would be hurled after Afrikaans children walking, sometimes barefoot, along the road near the rare schools that were set aside for them in the northern suburbs of Johannesburg.

If Afrikaans was scorned, it was nonetheless the language of legislation which ensured cheap black labour and heavy security. But the English-speakers would perhaps have preferred a language which was more subtle, less obviously demeaning, a softer glove to stretch over their own acquisitive fists.

For most of them, Afrikaans was worth enduring. It sometimes had to be understood but rarely spoken, while Bantu languages were for the most part simply ignored. In a suspended world far from the mine-dumps to the south of the city, in a cosy ark on a hilltop after the flood of empire, English-speakers continued to sip their whiskies and prosper.

THE WALL-CHART CHANT

Mrs. M. pulls on the ring of a wall-chart and unrolls a whole orange family, father, mother, Hennie and Marie. They live in an orange house, smile at each other over an orange breakfast, say "Totsiens" to each other and then arrive at school and the office. Still smiling by the end of the day, they meet up at home for a steaming orange evening meal.

Mrs. M. stands next to them like some pink plump Moses with a hennaed fringe, beating her wooden baton lightly against the plastified canvas and causing Afrikaans to trickle from our collective mouths. "Huis", "Dis 'n huis", "Hulle woon in die huis", "Hennie en Marie gaan skool toe", "Meneer Potgieter lees die koerant". At home I join the letters and words haltingly together. Next time Mrs. M. unrolls the family, which is orange for the moment but might soon be green or blue, I want to contribute more surely to the thirty-child frame-by-frame wall-chart chant which goes by the name of an Afrikaans lesson.

Never mind that Afrikaans isn't actually spoken by anyone I know, or that the lives of Hennie and Marie are about as thrilling as a bowl of porridge. I want to blend in, earn a gold star or at least a smile from Mrs. M. who tends to get a bit grumpy at her end of the baton.

The years roll on, the teacher changes, Afrikaans flows a bit faster but no clearer to me in the classroom. Still, even if we never do much more than recite the language, once in a while we are asked to give ***voice**** *to a song such as this one, originally sung by Afrikaner Boer War prisoners:*

> *My Sarie Marais is so ver van my hart,*
> *Ek hoop om haar weer te sien.*
> *Sy het in die wyk van die Mooirivier gewoon,*
> *Daar by die groot rivier.*
>
> *O bring my terug na die ou Transvaal,*
> *Daar waar my Sarie woon,*
> *Daar onder in die mielies by die groendoringboom,*
> *Daar woon my Sarie Marais*

(My Sarie Marais is so far from my heart/ I hope I will see her again/She lived in the Mooi River district/ Down by the big river

O bring me back to the old Transvaal/ Where my Sarie lives/ Down in the corn near the green thorn-tree/ There lives my Sarie Marais)

Perhaps the black blood of my early melancholia is woken in me. Perhaps the sound of the strange words secretly lodges inside me before I know it. The dark earthy sigh of the vowels, "hart", "hoop", "weer"; the rough tree-bark touch of the consonants, "bring", "terug", "groen".

Whatever the case, when it comes to singing the national anthem for the first time in Afrikaans, in preparation for the Republic Day ceremony in 1961 – which my parents keep me from attending – I am ready to lift the stopper of my voice and pour forth. (It is Mrs. M. herself who spreads over the seat of the grand piano in the school hall and presses out the tune, raising her baker's arms with a flourish between chords.)

'n

1963. For a year, I have been in England with my family. My father has been warned that he will be arrested if he goes back to South Africa. Whether or not I am in some way made aware of this, I don't know. But I make it clear that I would rather stay on than return home.

Still, in a vague attempt to prepare myself for the inevitable, I pick up a text in Afrikaans. To my surprise, I understand less than the bare bones of it. Have I really left South Africa so far behind? For some reason I aim my anxiety at the indefinite article, " 'n ". It suddenly seems so outlandish to me. Had it really existed before? What is that apostrophe doing there, and how does one pronounce the letter that follows? I try reading a sentence aloud; " 'n " sounds wrong as a consonant. But what else could it be? I take the " n " away and am left contemplating the apostrophe. The word has no sound to me. It has consumed itself from the inside, and the sense of the entire language seems to have slipped through the gap it leaves behind.

Back in Johannesburg, at high school now, the Afrikaans class becomes a form of slow torture to me. We have an Afrikaans-speaking teacher, who actually has ordinary conversations with some boys in the language. As far as I am concerned, one simple sentence will not join with the next, an anti-magnetic field stands between them.

Next thing, in July 1964, my father is arrested.

I go to school wearing the hermetically sealed armour of pride.

The blow is so strong, I try to convince myself that I have felt nothing.

My mind goes on ticking, through class after insipid class of history, maths, English, French, chemistry. I learn above all to take cover in silence, and work as diligently as I can.

But not when it comes to Afrikaans. I go into the classroom, sit down, and despite myself I refuse to function. Whatever I glean of the language, my knowledge is encapsulated, passive, unwillingly acquired; I can barely give voice to it. Somehow, perhaps thanks to my retiring mask of earnestness, or the disastrous result when I actually do open my mouth, or by pure luck, I am rarely asked to try and speak. And because I cannot, or will not, keep pace with the class, my comprehension worsens by the year.

One chapter of a story we read in class begins with a description of a boy kicking a tin down a road. Some boys seem to find the passage hilarious. I laugh. I remember that laugh, eked out of a fraction of words on one page of an otherwise only distantly comprehensible story, a sound sealed off from the rest of the world, like humming to yourself when you've slipped down under the bath-water.

How I manage to scrape through each year I do not know.

After some ten years of school Afrikaans, I have learnt how to recite, obey, haul my way from one sentence to the next about my summer holiday. And above all, when despite my attempts at invisibility it seems I might be directly addressed: how, without budging a limb, without flinching a muscle, to duck.

Between the apple and the tree

"Die appel val nie ver van die boom af nie"
says our Afrikaans teacher. The apple
does not fall far from the tree.
Ten minutes by car from our classroom
up through the dry din of the city,
locked behind an iron door
in a hill sits my father.

His prison is called "The Fort"
and it rises over the tranquillity
of suburban gardens, as my father
in his silence rises over my silence.
He is my tree, bent in his cell,
and I am the apple of his eye.

The one time I visit him up there
we sit at the back of a Volkswagen,
on the tarmac. The heat and strong hold
of his hand say more than all the words
we can't find. In front of us, two jailers
turn their shorn heads from our hunger,
count half an hour, then tell me to go.

"Die appel val nie ver van die boom af nie"
says our Afrikaans teacher with a smile,
and patient as a fallen apple I wait
for the day when my father won't be
quite so far away, needing no one
who uses the tongue of his jailers
to measure how far I might lie from him.

A CONTRARY SONG

By the time I entered university, the Afrikaans language was largely absent from my life. And since I left South Africa at the age of twenty-two, this could easily be the end of the story. But the end of the story tells me that there must have been more.

I did after all go to a shelf at the university library and open a book by Breytenbach. Apart from the enthusiasm of a friend, I think there might have been at least three other reasons for this. One was that Breytenbach had recently made a trip from Paris to South Africa, accounts of which were splashed across the papers. The combination of his anomalous political position – since it was rare to hear of an Afrikaner openly criticizing the government – and the romantic figure of the incendiary poet, might have whetted my curiosity.

A second reason, if it were true, would be more fundamental. I think that, despite my resistance, Afrikaans reached under my skin because of its deep link with the **land***, and that I might in an obscure way have been seeking this link when I went to look at Breytenbach's work.

The idea of writing poems directly rooted in South African reality increasingly preoccupied me at university. But on rereading my own words, I measured the distance between myself and the world which lay beyond the northern suburbs of Johannesburg. Nor could I truly appreciate the work of certain poets writing in English such as Mtshali, Serote, Gwala and Jensma, who in their different ways were voicing precisely those live-wire, despairing, language-bending street energies which eluded me.

Of all South African writers, only playwright Athol Fugard, with his precisely captured local idiom, pared down statements of loneliness, flares of humour, and assertion of black presence, seemed to speak directly to me from the stage.

In my reading I turned to Pound and Dylan Thomas, translations of Neruda, Cavafy, Amichai, Césaire, raiding them for words and emotion as I did when listening to Bob Dylan and Leonard Cohen. I felt that my life was enclosed in an airless glass ball; when I picked up a book, it was for an oxygen-rich transfusion of elsewhere.

If I could not find the words in my own language to name the alien world around me, then I also came to invest with inaccessible power those languages which were native to that world: black African languages, and Afrikaans. It was quite fashionable to learn African languages at university, and I did do a year's worth of Zulu. But the language remained remote and exotic to me.

Afrikaans was, despite everything, closer. Some of its sounds resonated with the Germanic side of the English language. It was a language forged in the blood and seed of settlement, severed from its native Dutch and grafted onto a local tree. It bore, or seemed to bear, aural traces of the place where it had been transplanted.

In other words there seemed to be something "natural" to the Afrikaans language, however unnatural the regime which abused it, and however inhuman some of its speakers might be. What if a poet could speak of South Africa in such a language, shaking off its sterile ideological armour, shifting its weight to reach a contrary song? I might seek out such a song. Of course it would be inaccessible to me. It would begin precisely where the boundary of my comprehension ended. If I hit against it, at least I would know where I stood.

Landgauge

My element is earth but my place was always
less certain than smoke in the wind.
I weighed my pockets with chips of quartz,
the pupa's copper secret, green canna seeds.
I peeled the leper bark of plane trees
to smell the pith of their bodies
rising from the ground; sat in the Afrikaans class
and listened, and refused to understand.
Yet I pushed against the words with my bones
and they broke open, the earth of their vowels
pouring dark as a sigh in the night,

"rustig", "asem", "roer", "brood", I breathed them in,
the rasp of cracked consonants against my skin,
"gister", "tok-tokkie", "treurig", "draai",
dust-caked, pungent, blood-burdened words,
raw as the red shale face of the hillside
where my road went, through a city that in the final end
would see us all turned into strangers.

THE OTHER REASON

There is another language.

It is not a language that can be avowed.

I do not speak it.

My life is surrounded by languages that I do not speak, but this one is different.

It is not a foreign language.

Or rather, it is not one of those South African languages which is foreign to me.

It is part of my past, of which I have been told next to nothing by anyone in my family, the past is still a foreign country to me and this language is its echo, a vibration I know while the words remain outside my reach.

Old people speak this language, it is a quiet code between them, not to be shouted in the streets, hardly to be used within a stranger's earshot. It is harmless, but must be kept out of harm's way.

It sounds comfortably chewy, like someone consuming chocolates with a rich, honey-sweet, walnut-bitter filling, in the company of friends, all of them chuckling over their luck.

The luck is not just because of the chocolates, it is because the chucklers are all still alive. I only come to understand much later that this is a language of survivors, what I am listening to is the music of survival.

On a map these people, if they chose to remember, might point to the exact location of the valley of the shadow of death. In Lithuania and Latvia, only five per cent of their number, that is one in twenty Jews living there at the time of the German invasion during the Second World War, were still alive four years later.[1]

If the survivors who continue to speak this language had not saved their skins, then I myself would never have been conceived.

My mother understands this language.

Sometimes before dinner she stands in the kitchen of my childhood bearing a blue aerogramme, her face all alight as she reads the words of the language to my father; I suppose he must understand something of it too. My mother's voice is excited with the tricky game of getting the words from the page to her mouth and from there to my father's ear. She is tickled pink, laughing as the meaning comes out and envelops her, laughing in the arms of this language and getting younger by the minute.

Her own mother has written to her, from Israel, in Yiddish, this other language, this lifeline of which I understand not a single dark and glowing syllable, leading to a place where I have never been, from a woman I have never seen. Yiddish is a language of history, of uprooting, of trembling and trauma and the laughter eked from trauma. It is a language of invisible history, though it has an earthy, almost visible sound.

I ask myself now if I didn't then, by some chance, hear in Afrikaans an altered trace of Yiddish. The two have a common Germanic root; it has been remarked upon that speakers of the one language have found the other, with its familiar ring, relatively easy to acquire.[2]

How would we know what sympathetic resonance we might find in another language, or why it might go on sounding inside us?

Do I graft something of the resonance of Yiddish onto the local trunk of Afrikaans?

Is this what I truly do, though it may only be somewhere inside myself, in a place hidden from my knowing self, well away from the malevolence that Afrikaans means to me?

My element is earth.

What hybrid language tree did I once tend inside myself?

We bury our secrets where we can.

If they take root, we might, even furtively, eat the fruit.

---

1 Dan Jacobson, *Heshel's Kingdom*, p.124

2 Joseph Sherman, Introduction to his anthology *From a Far off Land*, p.5

THE FRENCH CONNECTION

It was the European spring of 1976. I was living in France, my family was in England. I was standing on a balding patch of grass at the theatre complex of the Cartoucherie de Vincennes on the outskirts of Paris, steeling myself for an argument, in my shaky and approximate French, with a man who had parked his car there.

I was learning something of the actor's craft at a theatre called the Atelier du Chaudron, inspired by the presence of Tanith Noble, who had worked with The Bread and Puppet Theatre in Vermont. In my spare time, I had a job as a parking attendant, making sure that cars were left to cool in the right place while their owners went off to one of the six theatres of the Cartoucherie; none were allowed to drive onto our precious, tentative grass. It turned out that the man who had done just this was a theatre director, Michel Raffaëlli, more interested in my accent than my ungrammatical remonstrations. When he heard where I came from, he asked if I would read a few poems during a concert at the old Gare de la Bastille.

He wanted me to choose some by Oswald Mtshali and Breyten Breytenbach – it seemed obvious to him that I would know of the Afrikaans poet who, before his recent arrest in South Africa (in November 1975), had been living in Paris. This was a bit like requesting a foreigner who had never learned the first thing about good cooking to prepare one of his local specialities for an evening meal.

I was being asked as a South African to represent the poetry of other South Africans. Never mind the fact that I was white and English-speaking, while they were respectively black and Afrikaans-speaking. Never mind that I did not particularly get on with Mtshali's work, and found Breytenbach's entirely impenetrable. It was being assumed that since I was South African these poets, both of them alien to me, were in some way a part of my family. I hardly felt as if I had any family. But I was not about to reveal any of these thoughts to a laughing man in a leather jacket. He just had to tell me where to find the poems in question, and of course I would read them.

It was relatively easy to get hold of poems by Mtshali. But what would have happened if I had not been able to meet Georges Lory, and read the French translations of Breytenbach which he was then preparing for publication? I would probably still have done the public reading, relatively safe in the knowledge that few if any members of the audience could pick up on my (at best) quaintly inaccurate pronunciation. I would probably still have felt a faint thrill at the idea of being a mouthpiece for an Afrikaans poet who opposed the Afrikaner establishment; all the more so since this poet was now in a prison just next door to the one my father had been in little over two years earlier. But I doubt that I myself would have come to translate Breytenbach's work into English.

It was thanks to Lory's work – as well as discussions with both him and Adriaan van Dis, Breytenbach's Dutch translator – that I began getting an idea of what this work was about: French gave me a backdoor entry into the Afrikaans language, when the front door seemed to be bolted and double barred.

Only after I fell quite ill in the summer of 1976, and then embarked on a long convalescence, did I decide to have a look at the poems again, beginning with *Die Ysterkoei Moet Sweet.* I procured a thick Afrikaans–English dictionary, which I came to use for greater periods of time than a pillow. Within the space of a few weeks, I was hooked.

WIPING THE FOG

I open the book.

It's like when you're playing blind man's buff, and you're spun, and in the dizziness you have only ears to guide you, and the tips of your fingers.

I know the serrated edge of these words, the sound they make, but their meaning recedes from me.

They are a background, a distant floor, a rock-face in the fog.

They are as remote from me as the deep interior of the country I come from but barely know. They are perhaps dissident words, but nonetheless of the language of the interior.

Of a country which I have now left behind.

One day I will finally arrive in the country where I am no longer, by crossing a ***border**** *inside myself.*

For the moment, I am in another country, but I haven't arrived there yet, either. The words outside the window remain fuzzy to my ear, everything goes by a name which I have to earn. I cannot open my mouth without measuring my distance from the elemental touchstones of English words such as "bread", "house", "love". I am alone. Even the language of this place leaves me alone.

For the moment, I recognize only the dull, dim edge of the Afrikaans words from the country of before.

Or from a dictionary.

Then, gradually, from the images in the poems.

They float up at me, oddly twisted, physical, colourful, morbid, chuckling, erotic: air sweating white blood, man with bony wings, round fish in red jersey, rain like a veiled bride, delicate flower of pulsing ivory, dead feet erect as petrified rabbits, sweet potato runners with sore ears at a railway siding. I see them emerging from the lines of the poems as if the words were porters bearing them aloft, as if this were a winding, sonorous procession of paintings in the fog. I see the images directly, hear something of the music, then slog my way through the dictionary and my hazy memory to get the rest right, to find the approaching poem.

It is like waking up and piecing together a dream from a few surviving fragments. A salvaging act, from out of a lost language, buried under my own weight of refusal, under the lead-lined coffin of Afrikaner politics, its butchery and blind denial and dreary nostalgia.

Where the uprooted landscape of the past meets the unplanted landscape of the present, I sit translating, day after day, wiping the fog from the pile of blank pages before me.

DIE YSTERKOEI MOET SWEET[3]

Die Ysterkoei Moet Sweet was Breyten Breytenbach's first book of poetry, published in South Africa in 1964, while he was living

[3] Poems in Afrikaans from *Die Ysterkoei Moet Sweet*, as referred to here, are in the 1976 Meulenhoff collection of Breytenbach's poetry, *Het Huis van de Dove*. Extracts from these poems have been translated by myself for *White Scars*, if not previously translated, also by myself, in *In Africa Even the Flies are Happy*. *A Season in Paradise* was translated by Rike Vaughan. All other work cited here was either written by Breytenbach in English or translated into English by himself. The titles of peoms, all originally in Afrikaans, are given in English.

in Paris. It contains sixty poems written in blank verse, many of them of less than twenty lines long, but several filling a page to a page and a half.

The poems are set out in three sections: "Die Maer Man in die Groen Trui" (The Lean Man in the Green Sweater); "Kopatlas" (Headatlas); "Die Mond is te Geheim om Pyn nie te Voel nie" (The Mouth is too Secretive not to Feel Pain).

The first section introduces the poet to his audience, as if he were on a stage, religiously, tortuously engaged in his art:

> *Ladies and Gentlemen, allow me to introduce you to Breyten Breytenbach,*
> *the lean man in the green sweater; he devoutly*
> *braces and hammers his oblong head*
> *to fabricate a poem for you [...]*[4]

In this opening poem the reader enters the muddy, wet city of Paris, where the sky "sweats white blood" and pasty, threatening people stand at hospital windows "like angels in the furnace". Within two verses the poet is predicting his death here; by the third verse the reader has been invited to his funeral.

He is no ordinary man, since he has "bony wings". And this is no ordinary funeral, since not only does he hear the mourners, but continues to be riddled with pain and fear. Despite death, his "black tongue" continues to speak.

Other poems in the first section of the book are also preoccupied with death. The reader, after being presented with strong visual images of dead bodies, dead flowers and birds, is told that the poet "must still learn how to die", "must still learn how to go about it"[5] Some pages later he has finally made it, and, all the while chanting, uses a mitre to spray his own "carcass" with "holy water".[6]

It would seem that what the poet has in mind, as he kills himself worrying in one line and kills himself laughing the next, is not simply death, but ritual death. He is recording the personal **rite of passage*** of one who has left his country behind, and now finds himself in a strange, inhospitable no man's land. Perhaps the iron cow of the book's title echoes this change, an iron cow which

---

4 "threat of the sick", *Het Huis van de Dove*, p.3. Breytenbach's italics.

5 "death sets in at the feet", *In Africa Even the Flies are Happy*, p.4

6 "Anxiety ", *Het Huis van de Dove*, p.34

must sweat with inner life as if there were a second cow within it, at a time when Breytenbach himself is shedding old skins.

His constant thoughts of death are echoed by memories of the morbid stranglehold of the apartheid regime. There is mention, for example, of those "banished to obscure islands till the end of their days/ Wasting in damp pits down to slimy green imploring bones".[7]

But greater psychic space is occupied by the poet's personal experience, his combat with himself and the chaos of the imagination. He has left behind his old life, and its points of reference. He appears to teeter at the edge of madness. In his uprooting, distorted Bosch-like ghosts loom before him:

> *Then* comes madness like an armed man, and in a flash
> the walls whinny, chairs groan,
> burghers with hollow translucent heads, beacons of glass,
> dogs wearing spectacles, sounds changed into bats,
> theatre acts shatter like broken eggshell
> the bones of the brain penetrate the flesh
> MADMAN MAINTAIN YOUR PLACE IN THE
> COMMUNITY
> and fructify the deep land with blood spittle and sperm
>
> Since the pulse of a second reality beats behind this one
> and I die each instant floundering in the watery wake of my
> body[8]

The poet counters his own morbidity with a showering of fresh imagery. In "headtrip from fear to seed", though he dreams that a general has sentenced him to death, and laughing soldiers shoot holes through his head, he affirms that they will never catch him: "I am a ship on the arching waters/ my ears pink sails".[9] In return for his estrangement from the dark reality of the past, he has reached a shore of innocence, the lot of the stranger who begins his new life with the uninitiated innocence of a child in a strange land. This could be one source for the angel's wings mentioned in the book's opening poem.

By the end of the first section, transformation is in sight. The poet has earned his "doctor's degree in death".[10] Now he readies

---

[7] "breyten prays for himself", *In Africa Even the Flies are Happy*, p.6
[8] "provisional fulfilment", *Het Huis van de Dove*, p.43
[9] p.50
[10] "born 16 Sept. 1939, Bonnievale", p.49

himself for rebirth, one that is prescient given the circumstances of his arrest in South Africa some ten years later:

> one day I'll shipwreck myself upon a new coast
> under clicking palm-trees full of apes and parrots
> in the flat playful tongue of the shallow sea
> lie on incubator-warm sand
> watch those wandering sentries, the clouds,
> and as my head ripens
> I will grow new feet
> my africa here I come[11]

The first section of *Die Ysterkoei Moet Sweet* maps Breytenbach's progress from ritual death to the fantasy of return. The second section, "Headatlas", takes the reader further within an inner landscape.

There are a few playful references to Buddhism, and the Buddhist forgoing of the self. But above all there are glimpses of a world experienced from within the self, which appears to be in a state of intimacy and withdrawal. Several times, the world is seen from behind window panes, as in the poem "if a rider came galloping through these streets": "how we sit penned in with our music/ behind skins of glass".[12]

The poet is at a remove not only from the place he has left but also from the one he has come to. Within this geographical vacuum, there is a repeated super-positioning of land- or seascapes – situated in various European countries – and strange, sometimes mutilated dream images, painted in prismatic colours of the subconscious. All is seen in terms of transformation, echoing the shifts between death and life recorded earlier:

> he stands under the olive tree
> his face a glassy blue bird
>
> a rose-coloured man comes past in a cart
> the stumps of his limbs darkened with rain
>
> the sunflowers have chewed his hands
> bees creep through his eye-sockets [13]

---

[11] "headtrip from fear to seed", *Het Huis van de Dove*, p. 51
[12] p.63
[13] "log-book ", p.68

A woman makes an increasingly affirmed appearance, in the midst of saturated erotic colour and imagery:

> perhaps it's because you were a fish so
> red-breasted, your hair so green
>
> that it was always summer in my chamber –
> our bed a plumtree in september;
>
> like the time you wanted to crunch my nose in the fist of
> your mouth
> and I had to offer my flower to the oracle of your
> tabernacle[14]

However far within his own world the poet might travel, though, he remains attached to South Africa. The last poem in this section finds him turning from Paris to dream of the Cape:

> my heart is in the boland and will not
> be desecrated it is stowed away
> in a small box in white wellington[15]

The third section of the book, "The Mouth is too Secretive not to Feel Pain", teems with images of intimate love. This is a counterpoint to the death-steeped first section: the loved one is a "delicate flower of pulsing ivory" with an intoxicating "smell of life".[16] She accompanies the poet within the cocoon of change; she is his catharsis. In the landscape of love, "the trains are hungry but stay away like hyenas".[17] Thoughts of death, rather than sinking the poem in morbidity, sharpen the feeling of love's vulnerability.

Added to this is the poet's own sense of imperfection, a distorted self-image echoing thoughts of unworthiness in earlier poems. A note of self-doubt continues to ring through the last lines of the last poem, adding an edge of despair to the expression of desire:

---

14 "listen the raw season", *Het Huis van de Dove*, p.65
15 "ordain", p.77
16 "communion", p.83
17 "she is the catharsis, even in the white night", p. 93

[…] I stand on the bridge
with my disfigured self flat on the water
do you still think of me sometimes?
you turn in my head like a sombre tune
your white hands playing in the sun
my sheet is piping with dreams[18]

THE SCAR TISSUE OF STRUCTURES

In several works published since *Die Ysterkoei Moet Sweet*, Breytenbach is constantly aware of the implications of writing in Afrikaans at the time of apartheid. Afrikaans writers were traditionally scribes of the tribe, involved in developing an isolated, young language and bolstering the political purpose of its people. Breytenbach, on the contrary, describes the need

> to keep an uncivil tongue in the head. To write against that fate worse than death: the wooden tongue clacking away in the wooden orifice in order to produce the wooden sing-song praises to the big bang-bang and the fluttering flag![19]

This political opposition, then, involves him in a struggle with the language itself. He sees the simplest of Afrikaans words as ideologically tainted. For example, "if you say *man* (quite innocently) in Afrikaans, you are of necessity referring to a White. The language has other, derogatory terms for indicating 'the other' ", he writes.[20]

More deeply still, he sees the violence of apartheid embedded in Afrikaans grammar and syntax. In 1976, writing from prison, he responds to the imposition of Afrikaans as the medium of instruction in schools:

For we are Christ's executioners.
We are on the walls around the locations
gun in one hand
machine-gun in the other:
we, the missionaries of Civilization.

---

[18] "co la", *In Africa Even the Flies are Happy*, p.10
[19] *End Papers*, pp.193, 194
[20] as above, p.193

We bring you the grammar of violence
and the syntax of destruction –
from the tradition of our firearms
you will hear the verbs of retribution
stuttering.[21]

Small wonder that there should be a deep underlying lack of ease here, an imaginative resolve to break out of the containment of the poem. Breytenbach's freewheeling lines are edged with wildness as he slaps words against each other, alters grammar and syntax, bending his rhythm against them. "Committing poetry is a process of stumbling from breakthrough to breakdown."[22]

The result sometimes appear unfinished, uncut, unwieldy, the overflow of what Breytenbach himself, in *Die Ysterkoei Moet Sweet*, terms "die fontein van sêmaarso", the fountain of just saying so.[23]

If self-indulgence is in evidence here, then so is pleasure, a sheer overflowing of sensuality, sound making love with subject matter, Afrikaans free of its sexless straight-jacket, alive and well in bed:

heerlik hier op die bultende bed
saam met my
smul jy
met die voëltjiehande en goeie god
jou oë 2 buikige sonvisse in 'n waterbak

maak dit my hart so
soet o
soos 'n mango uit madagaskar[24]

delicious here on the humpy bed/ together with me/ you feast/ with little bird hands and good god/ your eyes 2 swollen-bellied sunfish in a water-tank/ make my heart so/ sweet o/ as a mango from madagascar

Surreal images jostle the mind, a source of "métissage, a new mixture of existing truths"[25] which changes the syntax of seeing. The human body, like the body of language, is not only fresh for

[21] "The struggle for the Taal", *The True Confessions of an Albino Terrorist*, p.357
[22] *End Papers*, p.151
[23] "writing now from back to front", *Het Huis van de Dove*, p.38
[24] "only for you this pulsing summerfruit in pool of juice on plate", p. 102
[25] *Return to Paradise*, p.xiii

love but also chastised, mutilated, rendered accessible to death. And this is equally true of Breytenbach as a painter:

> To look at a painting with conceptions of beauty and harmony (*etcetera*) in the head is to prance like a cock which has been taught how to crow the song of the times while being blithely oblivious of the flesh-knowledge of being promised for the pot. It is a scratching of the surface. You have to strip yourself (you have to close the eyes) to allow for the confrontation with the naked mirror which knows no aesthetic hierarchy.[26]

On the one hand, then, the knowledge of death and personal change, the nakedness, the solitary confrontation, the altering of the field of perception. On the other, the acknowledgement of the political weight, and sense of responsibility, that comes with working in the Afrikaans language.

Breytenbach does not deny the "scar tissue of structures" of his people which lies deep within him.[27] And though writing may be an act of exorcism, he continues to affirm his attachment to mother, tongue, father, land. Engaged in political and existential combat as an adult, he affirms a sensibility rooted in childhood. One poem in *Die Ysterkoei Moet Sweet* shows him settling down to write:

> light my pipe, scratch my dark flat brain for wordfood
> want to write poems in the convulsive Afrikaans tongue:
> womansmell
> of my first milk, grain of my father's finger-tips[28]

CROSSING THE **BORDER***

By 1978 I had completed work on *In Africa Even the Flies are Happy*, a selection of translations of Breytenbach's poems, amongst them nine from *Die Ysterkoei Moet Sweet*. Also included is the text about the daughter, the pumpkin and the moon, "Fascist Pumpkin", referred to at the beginning of this section.[29]

---

[26] *Painting the Eye*, p.63
[27] *Judas Eye*, p.124
[28] "writing now and from back to front", *Het Huis van de Dove*, p.38
[29] *In Africa Even the Flies are Happy*, p.113

I was lucky enough to meet John Calder, who had agreed to publish a selection of Breytenbach's work in English, parallel to publications in six other languages – including Georges Lory's *Feu froid* in French.

After Breytenbach's release from prison, and a series of meetings with him, I worked on a second manuscript, called *Hovering Dog*, involving translations of his prison poems. This was never published, however, Breytenbach preferring to use my translations as a resource when doing his own.[30] Previously, he had included thirteen of my translations at the end of *Memoirs of an Albino Terrorist.*

It was not only Breytenbach's work that I was engaged in translating in the late 1970's and early 1980's. Now that I was living in Paris, I was engaged in the process of translation from the moment I went out to buy my daily bread. I did not want to speak English any more, unless it was with foreigners who, like myself, were faced with the alien axioms of French culture. I needed the disorientation of strangeness, it was part of the rite of passage I had stumbled into, a dizzy way of emptying myself of the weight and tension of the past.

The French language was itself a key element in this rite, a means by which to achieve some measure of distance. With the help of my paltry school French I was just about able to get by in the first few years. I had no desire to study the language during this time, however. To me it was a tool, a lever, rather than a territory in its own right. With its help, I prised open a space within myself, within my airtight South African experience.

By the time I came to read Georges Lory's Breytenbach translations in 1976, I knew just enough French to more than glimpse the contents of the poems. Just enough, now that I had crossed one linguistic border, to sense that I might be able to scale the old grey wall separating me from Afrikaans.

In my mind, that wall merges with the tall, crenellated brick wall of Pretoria Local Prison. The letters I used to receive from that prison, several a year, arrived with a thick-edged oval or rectangular purple stamp at the top, dated and marked "GEVANGENIS/PRISON". The softly quivering, quick-eared animal of intimacy, branded with the sign of captivity. As time

[30] *Judas Eye*, p.115

went on, I started writing poems to my father, insisting on the importance of a world far from the telegraphic rational discourse which our visits were reduced to.

The poems were completely blacked out by the prison censor. Apparently, he believed they might be some kind of code. They came to represent precisely what I could not share, what could not cross the prison walls.

Now here I was reading poems in Afrikaans, written by a political prisoner, some from precisely those dim corridors I had glimpsed behind barred gates on the way to the visiting room in Pretoria Local. Poetry from out of that darkness, in a language I associated with the jailers, almost all of whom were Afrikaners; a poetry of transformation, breaking open syntax, sharpening senses in the face of deprivation, unlocking latent energies.

As a translator, I felt I was in some way participating not only in something of my own story, but in an act of exorcism against the strait-laced Puritan mould of the Afrikaans language itself.

A note to Georges Lory

(on first reading his French Breytenbach translations in 1976)

I was down on all fours on that chocolate carpetting of yours;
late morning, but there was an unmade bed behind me.
I suppose you had been translating a woman into love
just before I arrived. I had these sheets of poems spread out
before me, in the cloudy light from the courtyard window.

The words weren't very clear to me. It was like tasting
full-bodied inky wine for the first time,
or meeting a beautiful neighbour in the lift.
The possibilities were infinite but my leeway
was not, since, to tell you the truth, Georges,

my French wasn't that hot. Still I went on
from page to barely yielding page, out of the room
into the street, leaping from the meaning of three words
smack against the wall of the next four, rebounding
back over the ocean to the young man I had been

in a city with many mouths but a single heavy white
English tongue that everyone had to kow-tow to.
How our cheeks grew stiff with that accent,
how the whorl of our ears turned to stone,
how our one language was a disconnected phone.

Purity

Here is Breyten Breytenbach in January 1973, addressing the annual Summer School of the University of Cape Town:

> We are a bastard people with a bastard language [...] In that part of our blood which comes from Europe was the curse of superiority [...] We made our otherness the norm, the standard – and the ideal. And because our otherness is maintained *at the expense of* our fellow South Africans – and our South Africanhood – we felt threatened. We built walls. Not cities, but city walls. And like all bastards – uncertain of their identity – we began to adhere to the concept of *purity*. That is apartheid. *Apartheid is the law of the bastard.* [31]

These words strike at the heart of a system designed to exclude the "impurity" of true human contact across what was known as the "colour bar". Breytenbach is here engaging himself on the enemy side in an ideological war which Dr. D. F. Malan, Prime Minister of the first National Party government, had articulated thirty years earlier in the name of survival, using purity as a key weapon:

> From the outset the European colonists were far outnumbered; there is no doubt that if they had succumbed to the temptation of assimilation, they would have been submerged in the Black heathendom of Africa as effectively as if they had been completely annihilated. Of necessity they had to arm and protect themselves against this evergrowing menace, and how could it better be done than by throwing an impenetrable armour around themselves – the armour of racial purity and self-preservation?[32]

But if the upholders of apartheid are themselves bastards, by blood and by language, then their imposition of racial separation is not only inhuman, but an act of negation of their own nature.

[31] *A Season in Paradise*, p. 156, Breytenbach's italics

[32] Letter to Rev. John Piersma, 1954, in Leo Kuper, *Passive Resistance in South Africa*, p.218

Breytenbach spells out the multiple blending that has gone into the making of Afrikanerdom. Despite the Dutch origins of Afrikaans, this language

> was born in the mouths of those – imported slaves, local populations – who had command of no European tongue and who needed to communicate in a *lingua franca* among themselves; who had to be able also to understand the master. Not for nothing was it referred to as 'kitchen Dutch' for so long. In its structural simplifications it was influenced by the language spoken by the Malays; in its vocabulary by those of Khoi-khoi and Blacks. One can trace to some extent the proliferation of diminutives, the gifts in sound and meaning, the repetitions – so typical of Creole evolution.[33]

Likewise, he describes "the smelting down, the crucible's bastard fusing", out of which

> begins a smoothishness, raw pain's fresh metamorphosis – and how could it really be otherwise? – out of all those noses and arseholes and arteries and ovaries of assorted nations, those Nederlanders, Engelschen, Franschen, Hoogduitzers (of many regions), Savoyaards, Italiaanen, Hungaaren, Maleyers, Malabaaren, Cingaleezen, Javaanen, Macassaaren, Benjaanen, Ambioneezen, Bandaneezen, Boegineezen, Bubineezen, Chineezen, Madagascaaren, Angoleezen, inhabitants of Guinea and of the Zoute Eilanden, all of them using the Nederduitze, Maleitze and Portugeesche tongues, new blood will come.[34]

Using the same energy with which he berates his people for their asphyxiating ideology, Breytenbach elbows his way out of the narrow, historically false racial definition of what it means to be an Afrikaner.

What is more, he writes the Afrikaans original of these lines in a prison cell, breathing through the cracks of his inventory, in a place where he risks being reduced to a faceless number. And while he is at it, he addresses his own Vietnamese wife, classified as non-white by the apartheid authorities. In the following line of the above quote he writes to her: "Now do you see how deep the

[33] *The True Confessions of an Albino Terrorist*, p.353

[34] "on paper", *Judas Eye*, p.104

troughs of history run/ between your country and the one that is mine as well?"

So he makes the constant passage between the political and the personal, with the idea of purity perceived to be obscuring the truth at both levels. Politically, it is a purposeful form of blindness, used to justify repression while hiding the inevitability of metamorphosis. "Our nature is one of bastardy", he tells the University of Cape Town gathering in 1973. "It is good and beautiful thus. We should be compost, decomposing to be able to combine again in other forms."[35]

Elsewhere, on a personal note, and with his own particular blend of irony and vulnerability, Breytenbach describes himself as impure, flawed from the outset. In one poem in *Die Ysterkoei Moet Sweet*, "what the heart is full of, the mouth spills over with", he writes to his mother: "o I love you / o derided fig-tree / of the rotten fruit".[36] "Born 16 Sept. 1939, Bonnievale" begins with the lines: "Twenty-four years ago I tunneled from my ma's womb, /in my pa's seed there was already ruin".[37]

Death is present from birth onwards: "and I must live on/ propped up on my own death/ like a cripple on his crutch".[38] And if Breytenbach is subject to his own morbidity, he wages a struggle against himself: "writing for me starts with resistance: resistance to death".[39]

This same struggle is pitched against a political system which, in the name of purity, deals in death.

Baas

Many of the words "borrowed" from other South African languages by English speakers are connected with local territory. Words for things the immigrants had no previous knowledge of: words, for example, by which to name geographical features, plants, birds, animals, fish; also, food, clothes and weapons. Words by which to orient themselves, survive and ultimately lay down roots.

A reader of *A Dictionary of South African English* will find, for example, that "donga", an eroded watercourse or gully, comes from

---

35 *A Season in Paradise*, p. 156
36 "what the heart is full of, the mouth spills over with", *Het Huis van de Dove*, p.31
37 "born 16 Sept. 1939, Bonnievale", p.48
38 *A Season in Paradise*, p.256
39 p. 167

both Zulu and Xhosa. The animal known as a "gnu" takes its name from the Khoikhoi and San languages. The "kierie" is Khoikhoi for a fighting stick, with a Nama variant, while "sjambok", a whip cut from rhinoceros or hippo hide, was originally a Malay word. Many others are derived from Afrikaans, and in turn from Dutch. "Pan", a circular hollow in which water accumulates, comes from the Dutch word for a sunken place among the dunes. "Biltong", a sun-dried strip of meat usually cut from the haunch of a buck or ostrich, is made of two Dutch words, one for rump, the other for tongue.

When English speakers referred to other groups within the framework of apartheid, however, the words used often did not come from Afrikaans, or any South African language. The demeaning "kaffir", aimed at blacks, comes from the Arabic for "infidel"; "coon", referring to blacks or Coloureds, from the U.S.A., originally "racoon". "Coolie", an offensive term for Indians, is a word taken from Tamil and other Indian languages. "Picannin", from West Indian Creole, was used to refer to black children.

English speakers too genteel to use such words could take refuge behind blander, seemingly neutral epithets: "native", "Bantu", "non-European", "non-white".

But under apartheid, there was no neutral vocabulary when it came to describing the Other. And whichever word was chosen by those in power, the expected response was one of subservience. Towards a white male adult or youth, the word "baas", boss, was tagged onto the end of sentences. It was perhaps the most common Afrikaans words to be heard in the English-speaking city (its feminine form being "madam", or "missus").

To the "baas", a black man was generally a "boy", a woman a "girl". Only the baas was named in Afrikaans, but this word alone revealed the way in which English-speakers reproduced the patriarchal, feudal Afrikaner system of apartheid, also known as "baasskap", or "baasdom".

In conversation, "baas" was typically repeated several times over, punctuating the response of servant to master with a low, reflex noise the exact significance of which was not necessarily clear. At the end of Dan Jacobson's novella *A Dance in the Sun* there is a dialogue – if that is the right word - between the young white narrator and a black servant who has already used the word "baas" twelve times in as many sentences, concluding with a final "Ja Baas". To which the narrator comments:

> I no longer knew to what it was that he was agreeing. I couldn't have told from his tone of voice either, for he produced his agreement automatically like what is known as a good kaffir.[40]

If the word was repeated, and accepted, automatically, then it also masked what was going on in the mind of the servant. In other words, it was not only the expected form of humility, but also a means of protection; even potentially a weapon of irony, as in Motshile wa Nthodi's "South African Dialogue", originally published in 1976:

> Morning Baas,
> Baas,
> Baas Kleinbaas says,
> I must come and tell
> Baas that,
> Baas Ben's Baasboy says,
> Baas Ben want to see
> Baas Kleinbaas if
> Baas don't use
> Baas Kleinbaas,
> Baas.[41]

(Kleinbaas: farmer's son, or sub-manager. Baasboy: head labourer). The poem goes on like this for a further 78 lines, ending:

> If Baas Ben
> Baas Kleinbaas,
> Baas Ben must come and see
> Baas Kleinbaas there,
> Baas Ben.
> Baas Be-ne...
> Baas Ben
> Goodbye
> Baas Ben.

---

[40] *A Dance in the Sun*, p.200

[41] In Hirson (ed.), *The Lava of this Land*, p.122

The speaker himself seems by means of repetition to have not only lulled the listener into a kind of sleep, but also subverted the term "baas" itself, repeating it till the message takes second place while the long "aa" comes to sound like the "baa" of a sheep, or perhaps even "arse", or the two together. One way or another, the final "Goodbye/ Baas Ben" is not a little triumphant: the messenger has secretly delivered himself of a load of subservience and can now walk away, if not free then at least considerably lighter.

Anthem

From 1938 to 1960, South Africa had two national anthems, "God Save the King (or Queen)", and "Die Stem", whose words are the first six lines of a poem by C.J.Langenhoven, "Die Stem van Suid-Afrika" (The Voice of South Africa). From 1957, four years before South Africa became a republic, until 1994, when it became a democracy, "Die Stem" was the only national anthem.

As of 1961, we had to sing it at school assembly, sometimes in Afrikaans, more usually in English ("The Call of South Africa"), coupled with The Lord's Prayer:

> Ringing out from our blue heavens,
> from our deep seas breaking round;
> over everlasting mountains
> where the echoing crags resound;
>
> from our plains where creaking wagons
> cut their trails into the earth,
> calls the spirit of our country,
> of the land that gave us birth.
>
> At thy call we shall not falter,
> firm and steadfast we shall stand,
> at thy will to live or perish,
> O South Africa dear land.

Having situated ourselves in relation to the heavens and the land, we were considered to be ready to start the day. I doubt that many of us thought twice about the words of the anthem we chanted. The "we" of the third verse was no doubt generally considered to be white, all-inclusively white, as was the tone of the anthem as a whole. Apart, that is, from the mention of wagons, ox-wagons in fact, which as we all knew were icons of Afrikaner colonization of the South African interior during the Great Trek of the 1830's. This became even more palpable when we sang about "die kreun van ossewa" (the groan of the ox-wagon) in the Afrikaans version of the anthem.

At the end of the nineteenth century, following the discovery of diamonds and gold in the interior of the country, the British defeated the Afrikaners during the Boer War (1899-1902). The English-speaking community, maintaining the old ties of Empire, still held the nation's purse-strings under apartheid. Whatever this community's relatively "liberal" leanings, it largely benefited from the policy of apartheid.

And when its children came to pledge their national allegiance, they did so by way of an Afrikaner song. The "voice" of this song, though subdued in the anthem, is in fact resolutely an Afrikaner voice, as becomes flagrant if one reads the eleventh and twelth lines of Langenhoven's original poem (which we were not shown at school):

> Vaderland! Ons sal die adel van jou naam met ere dra:
> Waar en trou, as Afrikaners – kinders van Suid-Afrika.[42]
>
> (Fatherland! We shall wear the nobility of your name with honour:
> True and loyal, as Afrikaners – children of South Africa.)

The poem leaves no room for any other voice, it is as exclusive as the policy of apartheid itself. Just as the heart of South African history, when taught in the classroom, was the history of the establishment of the Afrikaner state, muting an English-speaking perspective, so the anthem, by way of a subtle detail, side-lined the non-Afrikaner singer. Our pledge of allegiance was both an

---

[42] Opperman (ed.), *Groot Verseboek*, p.95

act of collusion, and, if not self-exclusion, then at least part of that subtle process whereby English-speakers were distanced from key symbols of Afrikaner power.

As of 20th April 1994 parts of "Die Stem", in English and Afrikaans, have been added to "Nkosi Sikelel'iAfrika", in both isiXhosa and seSotho, to form a new, hybrid national anthem. But the words have been altered. There is a call for unity and freedom in the place of the creaking ox-wagons, which have now completely disappeared.

Voice

Writing in 1975, the year before the schoolchildren of Soweto and then elsewhere in the country took to the streets in protest against the use of Afrikaans in the classroom, Wopko Jensma opens his poem "Spanner in the (What?) Works" with the following lines:

> i was born 26 july 1939 in ventersdorp
> i found myself in a situation
>
> i was born 26 july 1939 in sophiatown
> i found myself in a situation
>
> i was born 26 july 1939 in district six
> i found myself in a situation
>
> i was born 26 july 1939 in welkom
> i found myself in a situation[43]

The first "i" here is autobiographical. The other three presumably refer to imaginary counterparts of the writer, all of them born in areas associated with disaster. Sophiatown was a black township taken over by whites in the late 1950's, District Six a coloured township razed to the ground in the late 1960's, Welkom an Orange Free State town beset with mining accidents. Jensma throws his personal landscape open to these different places before returning to himself at the heart of the poem:[44]

[43] *i must show you my clippings*, p.6
[44] p.7

i hope to live to the age of sixty
i hope to leave some evidence
that i inhabited this world
that i sensed my situation
that i created something
out of my situation
out of my life
that i lived
as human
alive
i

This triangular segment of text, by a writer who was also a visual artist constantly aware of the layout of his poems on the page, looks like the thin metal blade of a Stanley knife. Thrust from above, it narrows down to the final "i", which could be a cutting edge but also risks being cut off, utterly alone at its tip. At the same time, this "i" is multiple, one of those born in 1939 in various fragments of the country, their deaths (or perhaps those of yet another four) imagined at the end of the poem. One voice contains, and divides to seek out other, scattered voices, while at the same time standing alone, stripped to a state of sheer vulnerability.

"Spanner in the (What?) Works could be set next to a poem written in the wake of the Soweto riots by Oupa Thando Mthimkulu, "Like a Wheel":

This thing is like a wheel
It turns
Today it's me
Tomorrow it's you
Today I'm hungry
Tomorrow it's you

Today I'm hungry
Tomorrow it's you
Today I'm homeless
Tomorrow it's you

Today I'm in prison
Tomorrow it's you

This thing is like a wheel[45]

In a landscape of shared desolation, one person's life comes to echo another's. The poem works cumulatively, creating in words the same circular motion it speaks of. By the end, both the "I" and the "you" have become two halves of a potential "we", caught up in the motion of the wheel, just as today and tomorrow turn into a single day without respite. There is no truly separate first person singular here, but a multiplying number of participants, the drone of their song growing under hostile pressures.

Both these poems are works of virtual polyphony, in which other voices are invited to enter the text. Both act against political isolation and silence, using the pared down language of survival to build up an intense physical presence on the page. Robert Berold refers to such work as "the printed poetry of voice",[46] a mode bringing Jensma, a white poet, closer to a black poet such as Mthimkulu, able to combine a personal voice with an oral tradition of chant forms to express shared difficulty.

Land

In 1913, in terms of the Natives' Land Act, black land ownership was limited to 6% of South African territory (enlarged to 13% in 1936). "Awaking on Friday morning, June 20, 1913, the South African native found himself, not actually a slave, but a pariah in the land of his birth".[47] "Yes, we fold up our knees/ It's impossible to stretch out/ Because the land has been hedged in".[48]

The land: a way of speaking about the breakdown of human relations under apartheid; a mirror image of the human drama taking place at its surface. Instead of the country's expansive beauty, an inaccessible zone of rejection appears to the (white) dissident observer: "Now you are fought over/ negotiated divided paddocked sold stolen mortgaged/ I want to go underground with

[45] Staffrider, Vol.1 No.1, 1978, p.21
[46] "On Editing a Poetry Magazine", *Comment*, 10, Summer 1992, p.7
[47] Sol T. Plaatje, *Native Life in South Africa*, p.21
[48] St. J. Page Yako, "The Contraction and Enclosure of the Land", in Kavanagh and Qangule (eds.) *The Making of a Servant*, p.3, tr. from the Xhosa by the editors

you land/ land that would not have me/ land that never belonged to me/ land that I love more fruitlessly than before".[49]

Within the (white) dissident poet there is a war of love for the land, an emotional bloodletting which is also an act of planting, a rooting of the song, an animal movement underground, below the present dispensation. "I want my death/ to be a mole / that burrows, ever burrows/ under the property of your beliefs // so that you/ cannot find me, so that/ you cannot purge me/ from the soil on which you stand".[50]

You South Africans abroad, a friend says to me. You can't stop talking about the land, the beauty of this place and that place. I don't know any other group of people, she tells me, who seem so attached to the land itself, you are like stalks that have been snapped off, leaving their roots behind.

The poet returns to his country after a long absence, and struggles like an old lover to enter the bed of the land once more. He might enter her pain, but he cannot share her life: "My land my land o anus full of blood/ and love like a stiff body within the body.../ that day we rode out like the blind/ crossing the land again and again/ the flames of the sky licking through the panes/ we are blue and dying and life lies outside/ : I have died a little"[51]

Whichever way each poem is angled, it is the writer's restlessness which emerges, an agitated lover seeking communion in the face of rejection, blind animal bent on a deepening political path, while like an eloquent queen trailing an old blood-soaked robe, the land grows in symbolic power, and can only be denied at the cost of the song itself.

Border

A man past his prime lives alone in a border settlement. Members of a nomadic people make seasonal journeys back and forth across

[49] Antjie Krog, "land", *Down to my Last Skin*, p.114 , tr. from the Afrikaans by Karen Press

[50] Kelwyn Sole, "The National Question", *Projections in the Past Tense*, p.127

[51] Breyten Breytenbach, "journey (:I have died a little)", *In Africa Even the Flies are Happy* , p.79 – a poem which both cites and pitches itself against the national anthem.

the nearby frontier. The military authorities, perceiving these "barbarians" to be a threat, capture and interrogate some of them, including a young woman. Her ankles are broken by soldiers, her eyes half-blinded in the presence of her father, who is tortured and dies in detention.

The man opens his door to this young woman. His attentions to her are ambivalent. He wants to heal her, while his desire for her comes and goes. She mutely allows him to undress her, but reveals almost nothing of herself.

This man is the ageing magistrate in J.M.Coetzee's *Waiting For the Barbarians*, an administrator of what the military authorities term "the first line of defence of the Empire".[52] From the outset of the story he walks a solitary path. He maintains a moral distance from the tenets of empire. The woman he chooses is potentially an enemy. She in turn withholds her intimacy from him. Frustrated, he casts over her mute presence "one net of meaning after another".[53] In a way, she resembles the frontier itself, as she lies naked beside him.

Across her buttocks he discovers "a phantom criss-cross of ridges under the skin",[54] prefiguring his later ascent of the geographical frontier: "a series of rocky ridges to a low plateau, where we begin to meet with hummocks of withered winter grass".[55] Nor can he cross this frontier: "With this woman it is as if there is no interior, only a surface across which I hunt back and forth seeking entry".[56]

The magistrate asks himself if this relationship has any meaning outside his own quest. "Is it she I want or the traces of a history her body bears?".[57] Unable to embrace the woman fully, pushing from himself the history of empire, finding out ultimately that the young woman had found him to be "always somewhere else"[58], he is overcome with a feeling of desolation. His life is hemmed in by an inability to reach over to others, or find any semblance of reciprocated love, like the hot bread with a broken crust which the young woman holds out to him in a dream.[59]

In 1980, the year in which *Waiting for the Barbarians* came out, Shabir Banoobhai published this poem:

---

52 *Waiting for the Barbarians*, p.50
53 p.81
54 p.31
55 p.65
56 p.43
57 p.64
58 p.152
59 p. 109

the border

is as far
as the black man
who walks alongside you

as secure
as your door
against the unwanted knock[60]

Imagine the feet of the man in the poem, tracing out a border wherever he walks, so that the street itself is constantly divided as it passes through the white apartheid settlement, the stillness of the suburbs. Deep cracks appear in the tar, dark as the suspicion of a customs officer. Everywhere against the sky there are invisible signs asking if anyone has anything to declare, the border gapes open and closes behind the black walker in his shifting, separate country.

The whites take serene refuge in their homes. At night the pressure begins building up at their doors.

Rite of passage

The anthropologist Arnold van Gennep sees rites of passage as going through three schematic stages: separation from a previous state, the crossing of a no man's land of change and preparation, and then re-entry into society in a newly transformed state.[61] Of these, Breytenbach has always resolutely situated himself in the second stage, the no man's land, sometimes imagined as a desert, outside of the place he loves, or imprisoned within it:

> you try to extend your means and your frontiers, you transport your consciousness and like the dog having to define yourself you squirt a measure of it against this barred door or over that blind wall. Mobility is important. To vibrate in absence of any integration with a landscape.[62]

---

[60] "the border", *echoes of my other self*, p.37
[61] *The Rites of Passage*, p.11
[62] *Notes of Bird*, p.14. Breytenbach is here describing the act of painting.

No man's land: place of separation, change, preparation, where the no-person tries on various identities, where "a mask called Breytenbach"[63] is only one of the writer's multiple possibilities. (It is tempting to see in Breytenbach's paintings of men with blank mirror images an emanation of the poet's twin brother who died at birth.)[64]

Nomad's land: where one travels between the borders of different selves. "Whoever passes [between a neutral zone such as a desert and a socially well-defined territory] finds himself physically and magico-religiously in a special situation for a certain length of time: he wavers between two worlds".[65]

Thirty-nine years after *Die Ysterkoei Moet Sweet*, Breytenbach published an account of a journey he made to South Africa in 1991. Nelson Mandela had been released, and sat at the negotiating table with F.W. de Klerk. The possibility of participating in the process of transformation from within seemed to be wide open. But Breytenbach chose otherwise, concluding that

> I lost my friends and my sense of direction, I discarded my dreams, I scuttled my chances of participating in the National Reconciliation on the road to a New South Africa, I forfeited the repose of belonging to 'my country' with 'my own people', I deformed my past and destroyed my future. What freedom! An initiation demands sacrifices. Writing is an expression of the rites (and rights) of passage.[66]

What appears to be a passing stage in *Die Ysterkoei Moet Sweet*, corresponding to the uprooting from South Africa, has become a constant quest for displacement, detachment, a cleaving to the edge. A life of constant metamorphosis, that "infinite and goalless process"[67] is not unlike a poem, itself "a passage of the voice, of the breath".[68] Freedom is gained at the price of any proclaimed identity, though however much he might deny it Breytenbach's attachment to Africa, and South Africa in particular, continually resurfaces.

---

[63] *The True Confessions of an Albino Terrorist*, p.20
[64] *Judas Eye*, p.124
[65] van Gennep, *The Rites of Passage*, p.18
[66] *Return to Paradise*, p.217
[67] *Judas Eye*, p.125
[68] *A Season in Paradise*, p.97

PART THREE

Mourning is a Form of Pregnancy:

In a Marine Light
by Raymond Carver

PROXY

In the summer of 1994 I picked up a selection of Raymond Carver's poems, *In a Marine Light*, at a second-hand bookshop in Paris. I paged through it without being deeply struck by anything I found there, left it lying around the house, put it away on a shelf.

The next year, I went to South Africa to do a series of filmed interviews with six South African poets. I took with me another copy of Carver's book, a new one this time, to give to my friend Robert Berold. It was a case of getting someone else to read a book for me, by proxy. While recognizing that the book was in some way important, and wanting to share it, I was unable to read it myself at that point.

Since Nelson Mandela's release in 1990 I had read little but South African writing. I needed to respond to what was happening in the country. It felt as if I was somehow sharing in Mandela's release, and at the same time reliving the release of my father; as if years of dammed political energy had been unlocked and now reached into my Paris life.

I found no way to return to South Africa except by reading book after book out of the world of apartheid. Texts, many of which had stood on my shelves unread for years, now filled with significance for me: the 1990's, which seemed to promise vast possibilities for South Africa's future, also made the past freshly accessible.

I forgot all about *In a Marine Light.*

Then, in October 1999, my father died. Not long afterwards I reached up to the shelf for Carver's book, and blew dust from the pages. For almost a year I was, quite literally, unable to read anything else.

LONELY AS A CLOUD

My father had been having serious physical problems for years, afflicting him all the way from the crown of his head to his gout-swollen feet, confining him in the end to a wheelchair and sometimes, particularly towards the end, darkening his mind with depression. He was a historian, and doggedly, miraculously, went on working on two unfinished biographies. Then, in the weeks before he died, he lost the use of his arms and was hospitalized.

I received a phone-call, asking me to come to London. But I failed to appreciate the full gravity of what was happening until he said to me, from his bed, "If I'm not writing, I can't think". In fact, his inability to use the keyboard of a word-processor was like a death sentence to him.

On the second morning of that visit, I arrived in my father's hospital room, set apart from the main ward, to find him sitting up in an armchair. Looking not at me but out through the large plate-glass window at a tree-filled stretch of north London, he said: "I'm feeling lonely as a cloud".

His tone was quizzical, masking his despair. I saw him physically reduced in a way that he found utterly intolerable, confined within this overheated medical cell and at the same time adrift in himself. In recent times we had grown quite far apart, defensive in our barely expressed differences. But now he was allowing himself to speak of his vulnerability in my presence; and in a way that had not happened for far too long, something in me went out to him unconditionally.

STRAIT

Just opposite you as you enter Pretoria Local Prison there is a ***corridor*****, driven like a narrow wedge into the dim light ahead of you, shut off from the hallway by a barred gate. From this place come acrid antiseptic smells, blunt sounds of boots and keys, voices handcuffed to their own echoes. Turn left, then right into the visitors' room, where an ashtray on its aluminium pole holds burnt offerings of anxiety, while neon light dashes the stale air from on high. The room is lined with hardboard, punched with row after row of holes of the kind used to hang tools from, except that these are empty and dot the space like ear-holes. The walls press forward to listen, in their sapped green public paint that never seems clean.*

The room is sealed lengthways into two halves by a partition into which a few slits of perspex have been inserted at regular intervals. Through one of these, the visitor must try and make contact with the prisoner. From the base of each perspex slit, at a waist-high counter, a board sticks out at an angle into the room. It has been set there to prevent visitors from showing prisoners written information about matters that are strictly taboo. The authorities are particularly touchy about even the vaguest mention of politics, or any news of the outside world. Visits, they say, are to discuss "family matters".

At the appointed time, a guard shifts into place on the visitor's side. Like a customs officer of the heart he will make sure that all restrictions, including the time limit, are respected, and delivers himself of a few curt words to this effect. Then he goes off and plants himself to one side.

I first come to Pretoria Local Prison three years after my father's arrest, when I am sixteen and finally allowed to visit him at regular intervals. By the time I see him, he has been upgraded from the initial restriction of a single half-hour visit by one person every six months. Now this is down to a visit every six weeks for the same period; later it will be one a month, and towards the end once a fortnight for an hour. I am luckier than my much younger brother and sister, who see him twice in nine and a half years.

I set out with my mother, who drives us out of the comfort of Johannesburg's northern suburbs: gardens pillowed with foliage, plane shadows reclining on pavements, Springbok Radio urgently exhaling a rugby match from the edge of a patio.

From within this cordoned comfort, it is barely possible to imagine the visitors' room where my father will appear. One might even doubt the continuity in space between the luminous, lazy perfume of weekend suburban streets and the permanent dusk of prison. But there I am with my mother driving us down the main road to Pretoria, with the slowly seething cargo of my adolescence in tow, the anger at my father's absence more deeply hidden than a rudder under the belly of a ship. Meanwhile my mother grates the Volkswagen's machinery at each gear-change and asks me to peel her another naartjie.

There she is, parking in the shadow of the tall outer walls, walking with me under the striped orange, white and blue flag of the nation, pointing her nose like a weapon in the direction of the warders. There she is, with the strain of daily life upon her lean pale features, about to try and work out the equation of love and loss in this airless, alien box.

My father is ushered into the far end of the visitor's room. Month after month he comes in there, in khaki trousers and shirt topped with regulation brown corduroy jacket. He has lost weight, his face is tanned. For just an instant, it almost seems that he could be on holiday. But then there is the brave badge of his smile and famished light in his eyes, the despairingly long list of things he has to ask and say, and the guard fastened to his presence like a leash.

An extract from his autobiography :

> During the visits, anticipated throughout the month, cherished but so often unsatisfactory, we tried to cram weeks, or months into a thirty minute conversation with two warders listening to every word and able to interrupt if they so desired. Later, when we were allowed two visits a month from two people, the emptiness was not bridged any more satisfactorily. The separation of years took its toll and the divergence in our experiences made it harder to talk casually about family matters. As our children grew into adolescence or young adulthood I lost the thread of their lives and was out of touch with the events that shaped their values. Yael needed to discuss their progress with me, but I was separated from them by walls that were more than bricks: an entire world of experience kept us apart.[1]

Long after we leave the prison, I still see my father sitting opposite us, his face silvery with perspex as if wrapped in cellophane, as if love were a present that could not yet be opened. As if the state had some stealthy power to reach into the innermost intimacy of our lives.

Because though we have met we cannot truly meet, and though we have spoken we can barely speak. There are impenetrable moments of silence between us during visits. Even the longest list of things to ask and say will not reach more than halfway down the bridge between us, which is in constant need of repair and extension as our worlds threaten to drift apart.

Sometimes, when my father is led off by the guard who has been waiting at his shoulder, he is further away from us than when we arrived. Behind us in the rear-view mirror as we drive back to Johannesburg, the road narrows to a prison corridor that my father walks down with his back to us. The road of **absence***, *ultimately swallowed in a darkness which I, despite myself, push away from my life, since this darkness is a kind of death.*

My father, source of love for me, political struggler against a regime

---

[1] Baruch Hirson, *Revolutions in my Life*, p.10

of death, becomes a long-term inmate in a place the regime reserves for its living dead.

Some questions while standing on the banks of love

How much death can love dissolve in its waters?
When my father comes finally walking free
from the underworld of prison, I hold out my arms
but my cheeks are sore with a smile of difficulty.

If he could have left the dead years behind him
in his cell; if I could have emptied my body
of the dead man's smell. How much of the residue
of death can be scoured clean by love's

eager current? What do I know, standing before him
dumb and raw? If this is the father of my love
then where is my answer to his happiness,
why is my heart buried so deep inside me?

THE FAR SIDE OF THE STORY

From my father's autobiography again:

> I came out of jail with very mixed feelings. It was wonderful stepping onto the pavement outside the Fort, free to go as I pleased, once again in the company of Yael, and then of the rest of the family. However, such feelings merged with emotions that were diametrically different: I was racked with frustration and anger. The last week in Johannesburg Fort had taken me emotionally back to the torment of solitary confinement and my concern that I might be charged again was to plague my dreams for months to come.

Did I show both sides of my feelings as we returned to our house? Was I able to present a side that wanted to show after an absence of over nine years? Or did seething anger appear above the calmness that I wanted to display? My disposition was neither conducive to re-establishing my position in the home, nor to reconsidering my political position. Anger is counter-productive, dissolving all reasoning and engendering a frustration that feeds on itself.[2]

THE WITHHOLDING (late 1970's to 1990's)

I come to stand before my father at his desk in north London. ***Expat**** *London. He went into jail a physicist but since the family arrived here at the end of 1973 he has been a historian of the South African left-wing struggle in the twentieth century.*

There are books and papers everywhere, the shelves sag with them, the floor is piled with their advancing numbers, the air takes on their odour and the grain of their pages. The computer makes a meditative hum, its grey light is reflected against his face.

There is something I want to say to him. He is speaking about his latest historical research, on and on in intricate detail, I would need footnotes to be able to follow him precisely. But instead of questions I give him my listening look, waiting for a break in the monologue.

What is it exactly that I want to speak about? Does it matter? If we could only get back to the liquid flow of dialogue. To do that, though, we would first have to delve into the hard history that lies between us.

At school I came across the lines from Richard Lovelace's seventeenth century poem "To Lucasta, Going to the Wars": "I could not love thee, dear, so much, / Loved I not honour more". From prison, my father quoted the same lines to me.

It was true that life around us in the suburbs of Johannesburg was dishonourable. But how well does the heart nourish itself on honour? Did my father betray his family in the name of a higher cause? And can there be a higher cause than love?

"This inconstancy is such / As you too shall adore", writes Lovelace. My father and I have not reached this transcendent plane. Its possibility is there before us, but something would have to shift between us now to attain it.

---

2 Baruch Hirson, *Revolutions in my Life*, p.355

My father is armed to the teeth with history as I am with silence. How can we clear the air without some kind of confrontation? Surely our bond is strong enough to survive an explosion between us, the opening of old wounds to remove unspoken shrapnel. Is there not a Chinese poem about a bird that cuts through the sky but leaves no scar?

Still he speaks and does not listen, as I with equal self-absorption listen and do not speak, in an old protective habit of withholding.

HOSPRIZONTAL

By the mid-1980's the gout which my father had had since his early twenties started getting much worse, and in other ways too his body let him down. The physical world began closing in on him.

In the last ten years or so of his life, he spent weeks, which sometimes lengthened into months on end, in one hospital or another. His bones and later his skin never left him in peace for long. He would settle into bed, charm the staff, read and get on with his historical writing if his condition allowed it.

My mother would constantly go and visit him; sometimes, I went with her. It was impossible on those occasions not to think of the prison visits, his dependence on others to bring the outside world to him; the way he was left behind by us at the end of an hour or two, immobilized, walled in by an alien institution.

We drove away from the hospital as we drove away from Pretoria Local Jail, the car filled with his absence. The habit of it. The way there was an empty seat for someone who was not and could not be there, whose imminent arrival was going to be indefinitely delayed.

He should have been driving, my mother in the passenger seat, me at the back with my brother and sister. But once again fate was playing musical chairs with us. Every time the music stopped, he failed to find a place to sit amongst us.

My father the shaker and heat-maker, the sociable loner, the "one-man struggle" as his colleague Haleh Afshar dubbed him;[3] this man with his clarity and charm and power and stamina,

[3] "Talk on Baruch Hirson at the Institute of Commonwealth Studies, London, 14th October 2000", in Hirson (ed.), *In Memory of Baruch Hirson*, p.21

the sedentary **unsettler*** with an irascible will, his intelligence serrated with anger, was left behind us stuck in the institutional mud.

Until, finally, he could come back home again, to his study and his books. Back for as long as the lease his body gave him (and by the late 1980's he was constricted to a wheelchair), reducing the path of his life to reach between his computer screen and the past.

Back fighting for his own contrary vision of the kind of place South Africa could become, in the journal he edited, *Searchlight South Africa*. Back fighting his pain with multiple cocktails of drugs, while fatigue and depression began to dog his days. Back, until in September 1999 he entered a hospital for the last time.

MOURNING IS A FORM OF PREGNANCY

In the weeks preceding my father's death, I go into a fever of writing. I write in a notebook on the Eurostar between Paris and London, on the tube platform and in the tube, in the morning and the dead of night. I write while sitting on park benches, in cafés, in the stale heat of the hospital when my father falls asleep on his air-bed, and then later when he goes into a coma.

He is everywhere in my writing, barely any of which turns out to be worth much. Too much emotion surfaces in me now, along with far too little distance. But I do acknowledge, in the fever of words that breaks out, more readily than when I am with him or my mother, that he is soon going to die. At the same time he visibly recedes from us. While in coma he is fitted with a bubbling tube of oxygen, and tosses like a remote, restless statesman addressing an absent crowd from a balcony.

On temporarily emerging from this coma, my father tells my mother a dream. He is a prisoner in Pretoria again, covered with earth in the hot sun at the edge of a trench. "I will die if you leave me here," he shouts. His old prison commander looks on, two plasticine penises fastened to his jacket. At the end of the same dream my father is in a hospital, where a nurse asks what he wants for breakfast. But he wants nothing. He wants to die.

The living death of prison surfaces in his mind now, at the end of his life in the Royal Free Hospital, two absolute states superimposed in a dream just days before he dies.

At the same time, I feel the old, physical complicity with him return to me. When he regains consciousness for a brief period, and asks for three glasses of water and a hug, I lean forward and bury myself like a young boy in his arms.

After my father's death, I have the recurring impression that a second skin has grown over me, my body widening like a warm tent. My temperature must surely have risen, while it feels as if my centre of gravity has dropped closer to the ground.

Certain images recur to me as if I were in a waking fever dream. In one, a clock lies out in the garden, its hands erasing all lines and digits as they shave across the dial, leaving it entirely blank as they go on like the blades of a propeller, scything their way through the steel back, then down through packed soil, stones and roots underground. Time is not so much advancing as descending, day under night under day, just as the heartbeat does not mark the march of minutes but the repeated sound of emotion. Someone else must surely be beating the drum of energy inside me.

It is a state of inner heat fuelled by death, an opening of the ribs of the mind to take in a second person, a bodily axis liquid as the flame of a taper around which spirals someone who is not there, who is everywhere, expanding the palpable limits of the skin.

"Loss is nothing else but change, and change is Nature's delight", says Marcus Aurelius.[4]

It is a release from the dead-weight of all we have left undone, from our presence fattened with the inability to undo it, from the illness that has hardened and broken my father's body; a release from the final years when he retreated into his mind.

It is a return to what cannot be retrieved but was not finally lost, the memory of love come to increase me, calling out to me now from the door of childhood, accompanying me in a solitary song.

Mourning is a form of pregnancy, one body big with the shape of another, with the absence of another who gave shape to love.

[4] *Meditations*, p.146

Burial

1.

He is cremated.
His coffin
slides down a conveyor belt
at the push of a button,
and comes out as a bag of ash and grit
in a brown plastic jar.
Give me a burial any day.
Give me a sight of the body in the ground
and the sound of the spades
and the tears and words and warmth
of the living.
Give me a place from which to walk slowly away,
a place to return to in my mind.
Give those who come later a rock they can find.

He is cremated,
but for months we do nothing with his ashes,
as if the flames
had dispensed with death.
But then where should we scatter his
what is his
is there
no place on this earth
he could finally
call his
own?

2.

Home
is what he was
short on,
though no doubt he was
sedentary.
He brought gardens to flower,
even in prison,
earthed
his burning mind
among cacti, sweet-peas and potatoes,
then went and holed up
with his books.
He had ideas big as houses,
plans for Africa,
a presence proud and headstrong as a bear
trampling
on towards his **Elsewhere***
right there
in the half-blind ease of Johannesburg;
right now
rather than next year
in Jerusalem.
Don't all diaspora Jews,
like him, carry
in the transient, cubic volume
of their bodies
the dream of a country
that could be called home?
Meanwhile, children
are the ground
of their ungrown tree.
And so, accordingly,
when all was said
and done,
my father buried
himself
in me.

Delivery

The voices on the radio sound like fake jewellery;
music comes clattering against me.
I am listening.
My eardrum
is beating
but my body
is closed;
I am watching
but my body
is closed
for renovations.

My father
is in there.
He has just
given his death
to me.
The walls
between us
are down.
There is
some kind
of delivery
going on,
some kind of
increase
within me
without him,
some kind of
swollen birthright
we have
come to exchange
in the blood
of my mourning for him.

WHATEVER ANCIENT THING IT IS THAT WORKS THE CHAINS

In the months following my father's death I went on with my everyday life, teaching, writing, living with my family in Paris. But at the same time I was in a state of retreat. The outside world seemed to have become a place of clutter and noise, when I wanted a no man's land where I could mourn alone.

I did not get past the first few pages of any book until I opened Raymond Carver's *In a Marine Light* again. I can't say that I read it carefully at first. I simply absorbed it in a state of hunger, piecemeal; not as a series of individual poems, but as a language of energy, of understated muscular purpose that I needed to read, to hear, over and over. There was some kind of realignment going on inside me, an altering of vision concerning the balance of life and death, that was being addressed directly in page after page of the book.

Carver transmits at a low frequency. He does not bristle with the energy of projection. He speaks of and to the outer world, but he speaks of it without raising his voice, from within the radius of his own physical experience.

His poems are often pared down stories, which breathe like poems but do not indulge in poetic effect. They have little sense of **artifice***, do not create intense music, never include words for the sake of words. They have the flatness and directness of someone who has escaped for the moment from terminal disaster and been left with the foreknowledge of death. Each of them is a biopsy of survival.

Carver moves between statements of the past, riddled with loss and alcohol, and (beginning in the late 1970's) the affirmation of a new love, constantly aware that he could at any moment lose this too.

As he nears the end of his life, he articulates more clearly than before a level of perception well beyond this pendulum swing. For example, in one poem, "Energy", he describes meeting his daughter, who speaks to him of the disaster of her own upbringing. He is about to leave on a journey, he says, moving out of the bad memories of the past towards "the loving arms of another woman".[5]

[5] *In a Marine Light*, p.50

But by the end of the poem, as he leaves the house, he has shifted away from the question of all relationships, to approach a primal force underpinning human action,

> Moving toward whatever ancient thing
> it is that works the chains
> and pulls us so relentlessly on.[6]

The "us" is both intimate and impersonal, "the chains" part of some subterranean machine, the life-force that drives human existence and can propel one beyond all loss. This is stated here with a sense of disengaged clarity, a quality of perception that first came to me with absolute immediacy, and then accompanied me for months on end.

IN A MARINE LIGHT

The six sections of *In a Marine Light* each show Carver exploring similar preoccupations: memory, movement through the natural landscape to hunt or fish, exorcism of old difficulty, opening out to new love. But there is a sense of broadening scope within the book, as if ripples were moving outwards, from the self into the world and then back again, to achieve a deeper level of reconciliation with early days of poverty and trouble, as well as oncoming death.

As the book progresses, the presence of love grows stronger, gaining ground over the forces of despair. There is a sense of expansion of the spirit, suggested by reference to travelling in foreign places, to other writers and painters, and, most significantly, to the image of flowing water. This recurs intermittently throughout the book. But whereas towards the beginning Carver refers to rivers or oceans as places to cross or fish in, towards the end there is a merging of images of self and fish, self and river. The river in the outside world takes the writer with it, and becomes the flow of life itself:

> I drop to my knees,
> roll the big salmon onto its side

[6] *In a Marine Light*, p.50

on the wet grass, and begin to use
the knife I was born with. Soon
I'll be at the table in the living room,
trying to raise the dead. The moon
and the dark water my companions.
My hands are silvery with scales.
Fingers mingling with the dark blood.[7]

and

I'll take all the time I please this afternoon
before leaving my place alongside this river.
It pleases me, loving rivers.
Loving them all the way back
to their source.
Loving everything that increases me.[8]

The river which runs through these poems is also a reflection of the sense of energizing release experienced by Carver in writing them. "I felt on fire", he says of the six weeks during which he completed *Where Water Comes Together with Other Water*, the book from which some poems were selected, together with others from *Ultramarine*, to make up *In a Marine Light*.

In form, the poems typically cover a half to two-thirds of the page, raggedly lapping the right-hand margin. When telling a story, it is as if the content had been vertically squeezed, banked away from the wider swell of the prose paragraph, the rhythm abbreviated as Carver uses the limits of the poem to reach deeper into his own spirit:

We started down anyway. Jesus, please help me
out of this, I prayed. I'll believe in you again
and honour you always. But Jesus was crowded out
of my head by the vision of that rearing snake.
That singing. Keep believing in me, snake said,
for I will return. I made an obscure, criminal pact
that day. Praying to Jesus in one breath.
To snake in the other. Snake finally more real
to me. The memory of that day
like a blow to the calf now.[9]

7 "The Rest", p.174
8 "Where Water Comes Together with Other Water", p.194
9 "Wenas Ridge", p.89

The importance of narrative overrides any precise concern for the music of words. It is the rhythm of saying which is important to Carver, the voice of self constantly true to the self's emotion, here as in several other poems the need to confront and take responsibility for an old pact with the forces of destruction. His sense of economy, which involves the fearless, knife-sharp naming of events and actions, is determined not so much by poetics as by the movement of emotion within a wider arena involving the struggle between light and darkness, life and death.

This struggle is everywhere for him, in the earwigs he crushes when they emerge from a rum cake;[10] in the nosebleed of a casino gambler;[11] in the cod, dropped by an eagle, which he prepares for dinner:

> - cooked it
> lightly in oil and ate it
> with boiled potatoes and peas and biscuits.
> Over dinner, talking about eagles
> and an older, fiercer order of things.[12]

A sense of the relentless forces at work around him feeds into Carver's own inner pursuit, leading him to the perception of "an older, fiercer order of things", an absolute base-line against which everyday life appears to be relative, malleable, constantly open to alteration.

Through his poetry, he challenges the notion that the individual is permanently limited, both within a fixed past and a single role. Names are no more fixed than decor; one can shift out from behind them and become someone else; one could have done this before, instead of getting stuck like the doomed couple in "Next Year" who

> [...] went on
> thinking they were the people they said they were.
> Answering to those names.
> Making love to the people with those names.[13]

10 "Earwigs", pp. 103-104
11 "Blood", p.90
12 "Eagles", p.100
13 "Next Year", pp.54, 55

Carver's river, running through *In a Marine Light,* carries him not only forwards but also backwards, cleaning what came behind.

COOPED UP IN A ROOM

Carver is essentially a storyteller, whether writing a poem or short story, though his approach to his subject matter alters as he moves from one form to the other. His way of telling a short story throws light on the nature of the poems.

Carver's stories often take place in a house, or a single room of a house, barely connected to the outside world; a vacuum, with the hope pressed out of it like air. Entire lives are hemmed into a space that can barely contain them. "All of the objects in his vision, all of the objects in his life, it seemed, were at the far end of this room".[14]

The pressure between the people who occupy this space builds up until it borders on the unbearable. The sense of claustrophobic unease, the threat and need to escape it, is worsened by the fact that so many of Carver's characters are tongue-tied, as dispossessed of words as they are of ways to move out of the tight, working-class corner they find themselves in.

> Holly gets off the sofa and stretches on out across the bed.
> She goes, "Did you do it to her in this bed?"
> I don't have anything to say. I feel all out of words inside. I give her the glass and sit down in the chair. I drink my drink and think it's not ever going to be the same.[15]

"I feel all out of words inside": a physical sensation, described in simple words which do not add up to a simple sentence. The "inside" is cancelled by the "out": there is no inside, just as there are no words, only an emptiness which no character such as Duane in this story could put words to as Carver does with his inimitable, strange sense of economy.

"He is a great master of grammar", Geoffrey Wolff says of Carver. "I say grammar rather than diction, because the words don't arrest or surprise me much. It's their wonderful loopiness".[16]

---

[14] "Careful", in *Cathedral*, 1984, p.121
[15] "Gazebo", in *Where I'm Calling From* , p.115
[16] In Halpert (ed.), *Raymond Carver, an Oral Biography*, p.125

"Loopiness" seems the right word to describe the crazy, acrobatic but implosive way, at the edge of breakdown, in which a character such as Duane tries in words to turn his back on an inexorable cul-de-sac.

"I have to care for the people in the stories", says Carver. "These are my people".[17] He writes through a character like Duane rather than about him, not only through Duane's eyes but through his blunt and wordless butting against the world, accompanying him, embracing his desolate presence. This proximity is laid out on the page in lean, abbreviated sentences, packed solidly against one another, exerting an internal pressure, close-up physical detail taking the place of the words which people cannot speak to each other.

This is not to suggest that Carver lacks distance in relation to his characters, but rather that as a writer he enters a pact of physical identity with them which is unusually close. Sometimes, the act of writing itself seems to surface in the description of what the characters are doing:

> I stared hard at the shot of the cathedral on the T.V. How could I even begin to describe it? But say my life depended on it. Say my life was being threatened by an insane guy who said I had to do it or else.
> I stared some more at the cathedral before the picture flipped off into the countryside. There was no use. I turned to the blind man and said, "To begin with, they're very tall". I was looking around the room for clues.[18]

This could be a man trying to describe a cathedral to someone who can't see. But Carver himself also closes in on that voice, entering the vacuum of his monosyllabic subject's mind, both of them "looking around the room for clues."

So the writer uses the shabby, impoverished limits of the world he grew up in to generate the energy of his stories. Only in those he published soon before he died are his characters able to begin to shift beyond these limits:

---

[17] John Alton, "What We Talk about when We Talk about Literature", in Gentry and Stull (eds.), *Conversations with Raymond Carver*, p.156

[18] "Cathedral", in *Cathedral*, p.224

> My eyes were still closed. I was in my house. I knew that.
> But I didn't feel like I was inside anything.
> "It's really something," I said.[19]

PRIMACY

Towards the end of his life Carver changed wives, homes and drinking habits, seeking, it would seem, a force to sustain him in the face of death, leaving his previous existence behind him like a **refugee***. It was also towards the end of his life (between 1984 and 1989) that he wrote most of his published poetry.

During this time, he moved away from the mood of his earlier poems, published in *Fires*, which are still dominated by a sense of dead-end doubt and promise unfulfilled:

> Our future lies deep in the afternoon.
> It is a narrow street with a cart and driver,
> a driver who looks at us and hesitates,
> then shakes his head. Meanwhile,
> I coolly crack the egg of a fine Leghorn chicken.
> Your eyes film. You turn from me and look across
> the rooftops at the sea. Even the flies are still.
> I crack the other egg.
> Surely we have diminished each other.[20]

By the time he reaches his last collection, *The New Path to the Waterfall*, Carver's poetic voice confirms the deeper, clearer current of *In a Marine Light*. By this point, the freedom he has found in his poetry is equal and opposite to his own collapsing physical condition. As he develops the strength and generosity of his vision, he knows that, as far as the doctors are concerned, he is up against a wall. In 1977, after being hospitalized four times for acute alcoholism,

[19] "Cathedral", in *Cathedral*, p.228
[20] "Morning, Thinking of Empire", *Fires*, p.83

he was told he had six months to live
at the rate he was going. And he was going
nowhere but down. So he changed his ways
somehow. He quit drinking! And the rest?
After that it was all gravy, every minute
of it [...][21]

Gravy: a rich, flavoured addition, made of the essential juices of the meal of life itself. Gravy: the gravitas of knowing that death is close. Gravy containing the word "grave", which in turn hides the shortened version of Carver's first name, "Ray", within it. Gravy, piquant with pleasure at every moment won from death's clutch.

This poem shows Carver moving from despair to release; as he says in an interview with Michael Schumacher, it is release that poetry gives him, against the short stories and their pinpointing of constraint.

> The poetry gives me a chance to be intimate or open or vulnerable – or even surreal sometimes – in a way that I don't often engage in when I'm writing fiction.
> I'm more removed, more at a distance, when I'm writing fiction. I feel I'm much closer to the center, the core, in the poetry.[22]

Perhaps this is why, although he is much better known for the crafted intensity and innovation his short stories, Carver says in the same interview:

> You know, as far as I'm concerned, I'd be happy if they simply put "poet" on my tombstone. "Poet" – and in parentheses, "and short story writer".[23]

[21] "Gravy", *All of Us*, p.292
[22] "After the Fire, into the Fire: An Interview with Raymond Carver", in Gentry and Stull (eds.), *Conversations with Raymond Carver*, p.224
[23] p.219

Corridor (passage/passageway; U.S. hall/hallway)

Corridor: passage connecting parts of a building; passage from which doors lead into rooms; train corridor; strip of territory allowing a landlocked state access to the sea; route to which aircraft are restricted.

Corridor: a narrow place, often dim or dark, leading elsewhere. Relief might be offered by windows, books lined on shelves, a telephone at one end.

[F f. It. *corridore* corridor for *corridojo* running-place f. *correre* run, by confusion with *corridore* runner]: *Concise Oxford Dictionary*.

Corridor: where there may be great movement, intensified by constriction. A place of transit, where people ready themselves for the next station.

Corridor: U.S "hall", or "hallway", when referring to the passage within a building. Where Bill and Arlene Miller stand at the end of Raymond Carver's story "Neighbours", unable to unlock the door to the apartment opposite their own, which they are supposed to be looking after, and where each has tried to enter a different life. Where they lean against the door "as if against a wind", caught up together in a desperate embrace.[24] Their masks are down, like actors waiting in the wings; "between lives" as Carver says elsewhere, referring to himself.[25]

Corridor: a meeting place for those emerging from separate compartments or rooms; separate lives. A place between places, where a sense of possibility hovers.

In Alan Paton's short story "A Drink in the Passage", a young Afrikaner meets a black man in front of a sculpture on show in a bookshop window; then invites him up to have a drink – first wine, later cognac – not in his flat, but just outside it. Soon the white man's family is out there, too. It is illegal for blacks and whites to drink liquor together. The black man is on edge:

---

[24] in *Where I'm Calling From*, p.73

[25] *Fires*, p.13

> I found the whole thing was mad, and getting beyond me [...] with these white strangers standing and looking at me in the passage, as though they wanted for God's sake to touch me somewhere and didn't know how.[26]

The two men have run into each other, and gone up to the space immediately outside the white man's private lodgings, but no further movement is possible between them. The black man takes his leave thinking the other "was like a man trying to run a race in iron shoes, and not understanding why he cannot move".[27]

Corridor: image of the narrow lines of communication between black and white in apartheid South Africa, nothing but a single train line running between Johannesburg and surrounding townships, and only crammed green PUTCO buses available to carry blacks from their place of work to Johannesburg's Park Station. Almost no blacks driving their own cars. None of today's black minibus taxis with their whirligig-swerving across space, rendering it liquid.

It was a country "whose cities were linked by arteries... to make travel easier between one prison and another."[28]

Prison corridors extended invisibly across the land, injecting their darkness down the roads. No one was more intimately acquainted with this aspect of geography than the prisoners themselves:

> You are stripped bare of everything you can call your own, constantly stripped bare of anything that you make your own; you are stripped bare in an endless process of peeling off your protective covering and leaving you naked. So they can watch you. So that you, like the corridor, are without decoration, without covering, with nothing behind which to hide, with nothing they can't see into and watch.[29]

Absence (1)

"In some important ways we might be alike", Raymond Carver writes of his father in "My Father's Life".[30] Both men struggled with deep inner weakness, gave in to alcohol, constantly absented

[26] in *Debbie Go Home*, p.93

[27] p.95

[28] "Breyten Breytenbach, "Propos Détenus", afterword to *Feu Froid*, p.126

[29] Hugh Lewin, *Bandiet*, p.41

[30] *Fires*, p.20

themselves from their families for other women. But while the son overcame alcoholism and found a degree of deep steadiness, the father (also known as Raymond) died a broken man with a wandering mind. Knowledge of his father's chronic failings only seems to bring the son closer to him:

> He would like to pose bluff and hearty for his posterity,
> wear his old hat cocked over his ear.
> All his life my father wanted to be bold.
>
> But the eyes give him away, and the hands
> that limply offer the string of dead perch
> and the bottle of beer. Father, I love you [...][31]

On several occasions, Carver mentions listening to his father's stories, and being encouraged by him to write. What he does not countenance is the possibility that this same father's behaviour might also have been a deeply negative source which he would later draw on in his work. In his essay "Fires", he writes:

> Most of what now strikes me as story material presented itself to me after I was twenty. I really don't remember much about my life before I became a parent. I really don't feel that anything happened in my life until I was twenty and married and had the kids. Then things started to happen.[32]

Carver himself provides a fair amount of evidence to the contrary, not least of all in some of his poems. In "The Kitchen", the young adolescent narrator surprises his father with another woman:

> [...] This woman was, I swear, sitting
> on his lap, drinking a beer. A woman
> with part of a front tooth
> missing. She tried to grin as she rose
> to her feet. My dad stayed where he was, staring at me
> as if he didn't recognize his own get. Here,
> what is it, boy? he said. What happened,
> son? Swaying against the sink, the woman wet her lips
> and waited for whatever was to happen next.

---

31 "Photograph of my Father in his Twenty-Second Year", *Fires*, p.59

32 "Fires" in *Fires*, p.32

> My dad waited too, there in his old place
> at the kitchen table, the bulge in his pants
> subsiding. We all waited and wondered
> at the stuttered syllables, the words made to cling
> as anguish that poured from my raw young mouth.[33]

The words are flat, cinematographic in their detachment, the effect of the boy's anguish, which would have blurred his perspective at the time, doubled by the distance which Carver has gained in writing of this event decades later. At the core of the poem lie the father's insidious words: "What is it, boy?", "What happened, son?", a pathetic attempt at denial which breaks the bond of shared truth, the father absenting himself of responsibility before his son.

Just above the poem is a quote by Charles Wright, "What lasts is what you start with", underscoring the probability that this scene is autobiographical. It was in his poetry that Carver was able to reach back and unlock an old floodgate. Even in his later prose, his language continues to be constrained, filled with a sense of unspoken menace and blocked emotion.

In an interview, he gives a further clue as to how his father's behaviour affected him:

> I was eight or ten years old then. I used to wait at the bus stop for my dad to come home from work. Usually he was as regular as clockwork. But every two weeks or so, he wouldn't be on the bus. I'd stick around then and wait for the next bus, but I already knew he wasn't going to be on that one, either. When this happened, it meant he'd gone drinking with friends of his from the sawmill. I still remember the sense of doom and hopelessness that hung over the supper table when my mother and I and my kid brother sat down to eat.[34]

The absent father lodges in the darkest corner of the son's mind, love alloyed with disappointment, hope with betrayal. Nor has the father held faith with his wife. Whatever words are spoken between her and her children at the supper table, the backwash of silence will be stronger. Later, when the son sets down a page and

[33] *All of Us*, p.248

[34] Mona Simpson and Lewis Buzbee, "Raymond Carver", in Gentry and Stull (eds.) *Conversations with Raymond Carver*, pp.32,33

writes, his words will have to find the physical strength to survive that silence.

Expat

Is there any word more airless, more flat and mouldy than "expat" to describe a (more or less) permanent foreigner? The "ex" means "out of", suggesting a forward movement, but also hints at the idea of "former", which moves backwards. And as if it were not enough for the word to contain a cancelled dynamic, it also implies a double separation. The "expat" is defined in terms of a place from which he or she has moved, while remaining unpatriated anywhere else.

Just as bad, if not worse, the full word, expatriate, sounds like "expatriot": a lapsed patriot at a loose end.

In contrast, words like "refugee", "emigrant", "deportee", "fugitive", "exile", "alien" are alive with the anxious, wide-eyed energies of uprooting. "Expat" names the fate of the uprooted after the juices of doubt and discovery have run dry.

Various meanings of the word "pat" only add to the "expat's" unattractiveness. These include such lacklustre notions as "flatten or mould by patting"; "a small mass (esp. of butter)" as also "apposite or opportune, esp. unconvincingly so (*gave a pat answer*)" (Concise Oxford Dictionary).

"Expat" followed by "community" is even worse, a hardened group, integrated into its new world with the sullen vigour of an ingrown toe-nail. Such were the "Rhodies" of the 1970's, who had fled south down the road from Rhodesia. Ousted ones, necks twisted bitterly back to a place they could no longer claim as theirs, they were unwanted heralds in South Africa where most whites believed change was something you kept in your pocket for a parking meter.

Unsettler

As far as I know, I am the first person to have used this word, in the following paragraph:

He chose to have no burial, refused to come to rest; my father
the unsettler, talking to me in his measured, refractory tone,
walks with me all the way home.[35]

Definition: **1.** One who came, or whose ancestors came, to a new country or place, especially in the colonial era, yet who refuses to settle into colonial comfort, preferring to maintain a restless critical stance which needles local settlers and more particularly those in power; an uncolonist **2.** One who unsettles others by virtue of a restless presence and/or inflammatory ideas and/or explosive actions. Often a combination of **1.** and **2.** [UN- + SETTLER OE *setl* place to sit f.Gmc: see UNSETTLE, UNSETTLED, UNSETTLEMENT].

Note

The word "settler", in the South African context, has had three successive meanings. Firstly, it applied to the Dutch-speaking colonists at the Cape in the seventeenth century. Later, a Settler, usually with a capital "S", was a British Settler, especially one of a group of about 4,000 people located on the eastern frontier of the Cape colony in 1820. As of the 1970's, the word was used negatively by black militants to designate any unwanted white inhabitant of South Africa, as in the slogan "One settler, one bullet".[36]

My family, being of neither Dutch nor British origin, but Jewish, could not have fallen into the first two of these categories. By the time the third was really fashionable in some quarters, we had already left the country. But I doubt that it entered any of our minds to call ourselves, all the way back to my great-grandparents who had first arrived there, "settlers", even in the broad sense of "those who had come to settle". Nor did we in my immediate family think of ourselves as "immigrants", or any other such category that held the promise of permanence. We were white and South African, and that, for the moment anyway, was that. Being Jewish was itself a can of chicken soup best opened only on special festive occasions, and even then only in the presence of my grandparents.

---

35 Denis Hirson, "Gardening in the Dark", *New Coin*, Vol.6 No.2, Dec. 2000, p. 44

36 *A Dictionary of South African English*, p.631

Settling was something we did not do. If I try to think of my father's parents in these terms (and my mother's had already left for Israel by the time I was born), then I see them as stuck rather than settled. They were caught up in a state of stagnant, unspoken despair, out of love and out of steam, holed up in a lower middle class suburb of Johannesburg because there was nowhere else to go. The image that comes to mind is my grandfather's van, once used by him in his work as an electrician, ground to a terminal halt with four flat tyres in their driveway.

As for my immediate family, my mother would have been far happier living in England than anywhere else. My father, deeply committed to the cause of struggle in apartheid South Africa, was about as settled as the sticks of dynamite which his group of saboteurs planted under pylons outside Johannesburg. Not long after he received his prison sentence, plans were made for our move to England upon his release.

Meanwhile, how could we sit comfortably on all four legs of a chair in the suburbs, given his absence, and the situation which had provoked that absence?

Sensitivity to injustice came to us out of an awareness of what was happening to blacks under apartheid, but also out of our Jewish background, the one we had some difficulty bringing into the foreground. My four grandparents had left behind them the shtetls and pogroms of Russia and Latvia. My mother's mother had lost much of her immediate family to a combination of Germans and anti-Semitic Russians. Somewhere between the backs and the fronts of our minds, the shadows of these events went sliding, all the more substantial since they remained unspoken, dumb heralds of the wider field of Jewish history.

When it came to this history, and the notion of planting ourselves anywhere, could it ultimately be denied that we were of the Hebrews, a word which according to one interpretation means "those who cross over"? Were we not born crossers of borders, nomads in the way station of the suburbs ?

Still, any suggestion to my father that his position as an unsettler might have had the least connection with his Jewishness would have been firmly if not furiously rejected.

Elsewhere (1: Nowhere else)

Short story: a young white woman walks alone down a path through the veld. In the distance, there is a figure that ultimately attacks the young woman, falling upon her handbag and parcel, leaving her weakened and bewildered. No words are spoken.

The figure is male, and black. Nadine Gordimer, who first published this four-page short story in 1947, refers to him as "a native",[37] following the South African white usage of the time.

This word takes on further meaning as the figure is progressively invested with the attributes of the natural environment. He is animal – "he turned slowly and looked beyond her, without a flicker of interest as a cow sees you go";[38] then vegetal – "one foot, cracked from exposure until it looked like broken wood".[39] "**Native** [...] from *nativus*, Latin – an adjective meaning innate or natural, and *nativus*, mL – a noun formed from this".[40]

For the white woman in Gordimer's story, there is no one but herself. The black man is nothing to her but an outcrop of the veld and then a source of fear. The reader does not see her through his eyes, but to him she may well be no more than a way to relieve desperate need.

The title of the story, "Is There Nowhere Else Where We Can Meet?", underlines its desolation. There is no possible "we" here, the two protagonists being entirely absent to each other, apparently on different planes of existence. Neither of them speaks to the other. Nor is there is any imaginable meeting place for them, in this particular part of the veld or anywhere else.

After the man has attacked the woman, it is the place that carries the shock-wave: even the ditch and its blackjacks, the fence and, before the ditch, the tree that obstructs her, bearing something of the threat of his presence:

> the young mimosas closed in, lowering a thicket of twigs right to the ground, but she tore herself through, feeling the dust in her eyes and the scaly twigs hooking at her hair.[41]

By the end of the story, as the woman walks away, she thinks of the man's red eyes, and then, to add to his animal and vegetal

[37] "Is There Nowhere Else Where We Can Meet?" in Gordimer, *Selected Stories*, p.17
[38] p.18
[39] p.19
[40] Raymond Williams, *Keywords*, p.215
[41] "Is There Nowhere Else Where We Can Meet?", p.19

qualities, something mineral: "those cracks in his feet, fissures, erosion".[42] As if he were everywhere now, like the land itself, eroded under her own uncertain feet. As if, in ignoring him, she has ignored the place she walks through, absenting herself from place itself.

There can be nowhere else if there is no place to begin with.

She is left "an invalid",[43] walking slowly through a void.

His presence is a landmine she has stepped on, reducing her to this state.

Chinua Achebe could be commenting on this story when he writes:

> I want to suggest that in the colonial situation presence was the critical question, the crucial word. Its denial was the keynote of colonialist ideology.[44]

Elsewhere (2: Someplace else)

"There was this funny feeling of anything could happen now that we realized everything had", comments the motel caretaker Duane in Raymond Carver's short story "Gazebo", as his life slides into despair before his eyes.[45] The reader knows that since everything has already happened, nothing will. By the end of "Gazebo", Duane is holed up in the motel with Holly, the wife he has betrayed, refusing to open the door to customers.

Just before this, Holly speaks to Duane, reminding him of a gazebo they had once been taken to visit, by a woman who told them that

> years before, I mean a real long time ago, men used to come around and play music out there on a Sunday, and the people would sit and listen. I thought we'd be like that too when we got old enough. Dignified. And in a place. And people would come to our door.[46]

A motel is nothing but a stop-over, nowhere in particular at the side of the road, barely seen in daylight by customers who shift

[42] p.20
[43] as above
[44] Chinua Achebe, "African Literature as Celebration", in *Dissent*, Summer 1992, p.346
[45] "Gazebo", *Where I'm Calling From*, p.116
[46] p.117

from bed to car, leaving before their sheets have gone cold. It is the opposite of the place where Holly might feel dignified. The existence of such a place in her imagination heightens the sense of her humanity, while the inability to reach there only renders her condition all the more hopeless.

In one of his poems, "Balsa Wood", Carver describes himself as a boy after a breakfast row pervaded by "the smell /of burned brains and eggs". "I'm in a hole" his father tells his mother, "Don't dig me deeper". In the end, the boy needs to escape in his imagination and begins "to understand how it's possible/ to be in one place. And someplace else, too."[47]

Reaching "someplace else" becomes a necessity for the survival of the spirit; this is echoed by the words of Carver's mother, calling out to him in a dream in the poem "Son": *"If you want me to lose my mind* [...] *okay. Otherwise, /get me out of here"*.[48]

Writing of his own adult life in a third poem, "Waiting", (1988, p.185) Carver gives instructions to himself, road by road, as if reminding himself of how to arrive at the someplace else he has finally found. If the instructions are not followed precisely to the end, he warns himself, "your life will be ruined /forever". Every simple word is edged with a tenuous light, a car trip home changed into the journey of a lifetime, ending for the moment at

> [...] The house
> where trees are laden with
> fruit. Where phlox, forsythia
> and marigold grow. It's
> the house where the woman
> stands in the doorway
> wearing sun in her hair. The one
> who's been waiting
> all this time.
> The woman who loves you.
> The one who can say,
> "What's kept you?"[49]

---

[47] *In a Marine Light*, p.21

[48] "Son", p.23. Carver's italics

[49] "Waiting", p.185

Artifice

Carver was clear about the kind of poetry he did want to write, and the kind which held little interest for him:

> I suppose I'm not interested in what you might call the "well-made poem", for example. When I see one I'm tempted to react by saying, "Oh, that's just poetry." I'm looking for something else, something that's *not just* a good poem. Practically any good graduate student in a creative writing program can write a good poem. I'm looking for something beyond that. Maybe something rougher.[50]

His poems are not by any means uncrafted, but they appear on the page stripped of the outer wrapping, the smooth aesthetic sometimes associated with the artifice of "a good poem".

The notion of "artifice" is problematic, though. Derived from the Latin artificium, to make art, it has come to mean "a clever device; a contrivance". Yet a second definition associates it with cunning and dexterity (Concise Oxford Dictionary). "Artifice", in other words, can be associated with both the artificial and the skilful.

Tess Gallagher, discussing Carver's poetry, refers to the first meaning of this word. She speaks of

> the scarred patina of words gotten down on the page however the writer could, something wrestled from the torrent, using only that language which came readily, even haphazardly. Artifice gives way to velocity, to daring [...][51]

In another text she adds that "the truths he came to involved a dismantling of artifice".[52] In fact, it would seem that in his poems he was searching for a different kind of form, moving into a territory on the border of prose. This in turn might correspond to several needs. Firstly, Carver's narrative impulse elbows its way against the restrictions of the poetic line. Secondly, the poem is a combat zone for him, where he takes on old ghosts as directly

[50] Larry McCaffery and Sinda Gregory, "An Interview with Raymond Carver", in Gentry and Stull (eds.), *Conversations with Raymond Carver*, p.108, italics as in the transcription

[51] Introduction to Carver, *All of Us*, p.xxvi

[52] Introduction to Carver's *A New Path to the Waterfall*, in Carver, *All of Us*, p.319

as possible: Gallagher refers to the "increasingly unmediated apprehension of his subjects".[53] Again, he needs a dense but open space for this confrontation.

Lastly, "unmediated apprehension" goes along with the use of straightforward language. Impressions and actions, objects and feelings are named with a clean physical edge; they stand alone, without a tight clustering of adjectives, metaphors or other devices to bolster them. For all these reasons, Carver's poems naturally stretch out in the direction of prose.

Here is a verse from Czeslaw Milosz's "Ars Poetica?", which Gallagher says appealed to Carver:

> I have always aspired to a more spacious form
> that would be free from the claims of poetry or prose
> and would let us understand each other without exposing
> the author or reader to sublime agonies.[54]

In "a more spacious form", according to Milosz, a different kind of meeting is possible between writer and reader. The poem would be a place of dialogue, rather than centred upon the inner workings of the poet's emotion. "Ars Poetica?" argues for a certain forbearance of the self, a distancing from "ravings" and "what is morbid". Against this, the poem is seen as a place of wisdom and healing. A later verse of "Ars Poetica?" reads:

> There was a time when only wise books were read
> helping us to bear our pain and misery.
> This is not quite the same as leafing through a thousand
> works fresh from psychiatric clinics.[55]

Carver avoids the trap of self-indulgence. He refuses to see himself as a victim of the past, but seeks to release himself from its weight. Instead of descending into the inner labyrinth of confession, he lays the concrete conditions of a situation out on the table of the page.

His use of "I" is not a keyhole through which to see or display suffering, but a marker of movement between negative and positive energies. It is by exploring this movement that he creates a "spacious form".

---

[53] Introduction to Carver's *A New Path to the Waterfall*, in Carver, *All of Us*, p.320

[54] p.319

[55] Cselaw Milosz, "Ars Poetica?", *Bells in Winter*, p.30, tr. from the Polish by the poet with Lillian Vallee

Tess Gallagher mentions that Carver's poetry has been severely criticized, citing "those honed minds that find Ray's transparency somehow an insult to intelligence".[56] Behind such statements there lies a conflict over what exactly constitutes a poem, or a "good" poem, and further conflict over the uses to which poetry should be put. I imagine Carver arguing, with Milosz, that it should somehow help us to lead better lives, since it is written in the name of what is good "with the hope/ that good spirits, not evil ones, choose us for their instrument".[57]

The temptation, then, would be to set up an opposition between a rarefied, self-indulgent, stuffily conservative poetry, wrapped in its own intelligence and withdrawn behind artifice, on the one hand; on the other, a more vital poetry that, as Carver puts it, "should deliver a certain number of emotional punches".[58] Poetry open to dialogue, concerned with transformation within and beyond the self.

Returning to the definition of the word "artifice", however, this opposition is not always helpful. Artifice can be skilfully used to protect a rare and fragile vision, while concern with the emotions or the world will hardly save a poem from being paltry. This, however, is the way the battlefield was drawn in apartheid South Africa. In this political vacuum, artists were expected by some to play a political role and give immediate voice to the rawness of oppression, the ivory tower being perceived of as fitting neatly into the battlements of the regime.

Es'kia Mphahlele wrote the following from a black point of view in 1960:

> Ours is a fugitive culture: borrowing here, incorporating there, retaining this, rejecting that. But it is a virile culture. The clamour of it is going to keep beating on the walls surrounding the already fragmented culture of the whites until they crumble.[59]

The image of the wall, biblical in its reference and particularly apt at the time of apartheid, could in turn be applied to artistic form itself. White poetry was often protective to the point of being stultifying, the language of white writers laced with "polite

[56] Gallagher, introduction to Carver, *All of Us*, p.xxv
[57] Milosz, "Ars Poetica?", p.31
[58] Larry McCaffery and Sinda Gregory, "An Interview with Raymond Carver", in Gentry and Stull (eds.), *Conversations with Raymond Carver*, p.108, italics as in the transcription
[59] "Black and White", in *New Statesman*, 10th Sept. 1960 p.346

cowardice".[60] "Artifice", in this context, could be critically associated with the idea of a political facade, by those insisting on the poem as an open-ended vehicle of regeneration; one in which "Words are born the way/ nations come out of servitude."[61]

In the decades after Mphahlele wrote his text, poets began infusing the English language (as also Afrikaans) with a jagged new energy, contesting not only political certainties but also the nature and limits of the language itself:

> The English language, the language of settlerdom, power and commerce, is being shaped by African sensibilities and forms – African not necessarily meaning black. Increasingly since the 70's, and particularly since the unbanning of the ANC and the demythologisation of Mandela, poets are more and more using the living language, breaking the grids of formal political or literary orthodoxy.[62]

Carver makes no overt political statement about his poetry, any more than he does about his prose. But in one interview he does react against what he terms a "neo-conservative critic" who commented that "we shouldn't write about people who are dispossessed and unhappy, and whose lives have gone bust". The critic would have preferred Carver to "put a happy face on things", and in this context the writer's determination to write about the "submerged population" does have a political connotation.[63]

His search for "something rougher" in a poem gives a driving edge, not only to the act of personal exorcism but also to the act of freeing himself from a state of dispossession.

Refugee

> He had a very rough survival, almost refugee, attitude towards the world. He'd never leave the lunchroom without taking a package of food, which he'd store in his room. Many of these packages would go untouched, but it seemed as if he expected to be cut off in some way or caught someplace without sustenance.[64]

---

[60] Karen Press in Robert Berold (ed.), *South African Poets on Poetry*, p.16

[61] Mafika Gwala, "Words are also Born", *Jol'iinkomo*, p.55

[62] Robert Berold, "On Editing a Poetry Magazine", *Comment*, 10, Summer 1992, p.8

[63] "David Sexton talks to Raymond Carver" in Gentry and Stull (eds.), *Conversations with Raymond Carver*, p.130

[64] Stephen Dobyns in Halpert (ed.), *Raymond Carver, an Oral Biography*, p.110

In an interview, Carver accepts that many of the characters in his stories are constantly eating, and adds that "poor people, disenfranchised people, they can never get enough to eat. They're always putting too much on their plates and then are not able to eat it".[65]

If Carver himself was a refugee, on the run from the condition of his early days, then this might have deeply affected not only the substance of his writing, but also the form it took.

In his essay "Fires", he describes the world he knew best, and wrote about, as senseless and unstable, "one that seemed to change gears and directions, along with its rules, every day". He could neither find material stability in this world, nor believe in what he terms its "essential *correctness*". To write a novel, he adds, a writer must believe in the surrounding world as he did not, "a world that will, for a time anyway, stay fixed in one place".[66]

The forms Carver chose to write in, both short story and poem, were correspondingly brief. Portable as a suitcase, a map, a weapon, a letter. In this respect, he resembles those black writers in apartheid South Africa who committed words to paper while on the hop, if not on the run:

> It is impossible for a writer who lives in oppression to organise his whole personality into creating a novel. The short story is used as a short cut to prose meaning and one gets some things off one's chest in quick time.[67]

The rivers which flow through Carver's poems could easily carry a refugee spirit onward as he fishes in their water or sits and watches them. His favourites are coastal rivers, especially at the place where they run into the sea, "I love them the way some men love horses/ or glamorous women".[68]

But the counterpoint to the river in his poems is the house. Particularly the house where he sits writing in his later poems, a still place of reconciliation with himself and the woman he loves, as in the opening lines of the final poem in "*In a Marine Light*":

---

[65] John Alton, "What We Talk About When We Talk About Literature: An Interview with Raymond Carver", in Gentry and Stull (eds.), *Conversations with Raymond Carver*, p.163

[66] "Fires", in *Fires*, p.35, Carver's italics

[67] Es'kia Mphahlele, "Black and White", *New Statesman* 10th Sept. 1960, p.343

[68] "Where Water Comes Together with Other Water", *In a Marine Light*, p.194

Snow began falling late last night. Wet flakes
dropping past windows, snow covering
the skylights. We watched for a time, surprised
and happy. Glad to be here, and nowhere else.[69]

[69] "The Gift", in *In A Marine Light*, p.205

PART FOUR

Re–membering:

Je me souviens
(I Remember)
by Georges Perec

JE ME SOUVIENS (bare bones, 1989)

I first heard of Georges Perec's *Je me souviens* when the actor Sami Frey did a well-publicised one-man performance based on this text in Paris in 1989. There was a photograph in the paper of Frey on a bicycle, apparently going nowhere, in a decor of cloth raised by threads into a multitude of peaks. I didn't see the performance, but perhaps as a result of reading about it I did leaf through *Je me souviens* in a bookshop soon afterwards. I remember wondering whether any of my French friends knew about the book, since it was an inventory of memories at least some of which they might share. For the most part, I did not.

This was the first reason why Perec's book was no more than a curiosity to me. The second had to do with the flatness of his style, and the ordinary, even **banal*** quality which seemed to pervade so much of his subject matter. What he had done was set down 480 numbered sentences, or groups of sentences, each beginning with the words "Je me souviens" (I remember). This is followed, in all but the 480th case, which simply reads "Je me souviens",[1] by the briefest of notations of what it was that he remembered.

In translation,[2] the opening page of Perec's book reads like this:

> 1
> I remember that Reda Caire did a special live performance at the Porte de Saint-Cloud cinema.
>
> 2
> I remember that my uncle had an 11 CV whose license plate number was 7070 RL2.
>
> 3
> I remember *Les Agriculteurs* Cinema, the club armchairs of the *Caméra*, and the double seats of the *Panthéon*.[3]

Here, as in most of the book, Perec pares away the flesh of description, gives no hint of his own emotion, no direct idea of the link between his own experience and what is being remembered. Instead, he records each item in the briefest, most disengaged way

[1] 1998, p.116
[2] All translations from the French in this section are by myself
[3] *Je me souviens*, p.13, of which the top half is blank

possible. This procedure was not particularly attractive to me. In fact, at the time, it was precisely the opposite of what interested me about the relationship between writing and memory.

I REMEMBER (flesh, early 1980's)

I sit down to write about South Africa.

I live at the end of a cobbled, narrow cul-de-sac in the 11th arrondissement of Paris, past a boilermakers, several other small factories and offices, low blocks of flats and a crêche run by Scientologists; the first flat I have ever truly been able to call my own.

Opposite my second floor window there is a square, with a dull oblong block of flats to the left and, behind the sandpit at the far end, a prefab which serves as a club for old age pensioners. The square is lined with ten acacia trees. Its sand reflects the light, and is pale ochre in the early morning, turning rough and glittery as sandpaper in the middle of a clear summer's day, with a diluted violet stain across it as the sun goes down.

Not much happens in the square. Sometimes, unemployed men come and play pétanque, and I hear the clicking of the metal balls, or a man shouting out "Jolie! Jolie!" in appreciation of a fine shot. Once, on a hot day, the children of the concierge stand at the edge of the sandpit, count loudly to three, flex their knees and dive in.

The square is like a page, seamed to the page I write on. On arriving in France I had pushed South Africa away from me as hard as I was able to, wanting a new space for myself, a new language, a new skin. But now, after six or seven years, I want it back.

It won't come.

My words are all restless with anger, or static as anecdotes, memories of memories, dry as scars, nothing I didn't know before I started. My wastepaper basket fills with crumpled pages.

I become aware of a man who is out in the square every day. He sits on one of the three benches between the trees opposite the block of flats. Behind him rises a great solid wall of bone-white stone. His face is closed; the heavy, unshaven features seem to be stuck onto it. His clothes are toneless as cardboard or sacking, and he wears military boots. He sits with all his weight against the bench, hardly bending to its form, arms folded in violent immobility.

Sometimes, other people come up and talk to him. He even joins in with the men playing pétanque, but when they leave he returns to his bench, and possesses it with his bulk, and the whole square seems to cave in under him.

In the autumn, when the acacias lose their leaves and the light dulls on the sand, he is still there. His form is tight as a mortar ready to hurl itself. He has gathered the square like a greatcoat around him and turned it into his encampment. In the wake of his utter isolation, I imagine other men, mute and empty, massing to join ranks with him. Upon the sand opposite my blank page, an unseen threat gathers around this man, his presence swollen with news of rising unemployment and increasing support for the blunt, cocksure stance of the French extreme right.

With the sharp grey glaze of winter at the window, I sit for longer hours at the page. Eventually, some words survive my continual attempts to scratch them out. They pack themselves densely as refugees with nothing of their own in the world but each other, in paragraphs each surrounded like verses by a blank breathing space, in passages not longer than a page or two. Across these pages, some fragmented semblance of Johannesburg begins to appear.

The city has been refracted by seven years of distance. It is a city of memory, and I want it to sing. With everything I have learned from Isaac Babel and Bruno Schultz, Henri Michaux and Michael Ondaatje, Dylan Thomas, Pablo Neruda and anyone else who knows how to rub a rock and its shadow together to get a song, with my best breath I want to lever it out of the heavy place where it has sunk into me.

What emerges first, as if my language formed a convex lens above the surface of experience, are enlarged, palpable details: the molasses back of a rhinoceros beetle trundling against the inner seam of a gutter; the star-shaped leathery flower of the stapelia plant with its stink-bomb odour. There is the dark-stained wooden dog-clock sitting on a doily in my grandparents' living room with one eyeball for minutes and the other for the hour, and neither of them turning any more. There are my marooned grandparents, my family, my father and then his absence.

There is my grandmother Toba, my mother's mother whom I never knew in South Africa, the one I went to visit in Israel in the late 1970's and who informed me that our family story did, after all, begin well before South Africa. There are her animated sepia stories of ***Russia*****; there are her husband my grandfather's stories of being a foot-soldier in the Tzar's army, trying to survive the First World War.*

These stories contain a kind of atmospheric pressure gathering out of the past, blowing Johannesburg into a new perspective. The city that circumscribed the first two decades of my life becomes a way-station in our family history alongside other places, Riga and Minsk, Cambridge, London, Petah Tiqwa and Jerusalem, each of them edged with the wind of passage. As is Paris, where I sit writing the pages that will become The House Next Door to Africa.

On the way out one evening, I find the man from the square, bedded down in blankets and a sleeping bag on the black and white tiled floor of our entrance hall, under the letter-boxes. From out of his scrubby, reclining face he grants me a plain smile, as if he were a neighbour who happened to have just moved in. He is less alien at close quarters, more vulnerable, younger. He must be in his mid-twenties. I buy him some beer at the local grocery.

No doubt his presence here is more deeply founded than mine; I am the real sojourner. The most substantial house I know is made of words, words like the honey sucked up by bees when smoked from their hive. I seek words that contain whatever sustenance I have taken from the past.

Perec's Je me souviens, *when I first come to open it some years later in 1989, appears to me to be without any sustenance at all: on page after page, memory is reduced to nothing but a thinly illustrated rhetorical system of notation. It takes twelve years and my father's death before I open the book again.*

MOURNING BECOMES SOMETHING ELSE
(late 1990's)

Now that my father has died he feels lighter than air to me, released from the double ***exile**** *of politics and the wheelchair-bound body that would not let him out of his own front door.*

His weight falls from me like ballast, but the heat of his presence is constantly with me. I wear clothes that used to be his, hardly write anything that does not concern him. Still, he cannot go on burning like this inside me. In the end, flames will reduce to a heap of charcoal and ash even the tallest, broadest tree.

A friend of mine, Nina Bogin, sends me one of her poems, "There's no hour" which I read over and over, holding onto it like a talisman. Here are the second and final verses:

> In certain hours, my father keeps me company.
> His warmth comes to visit me from deep inside myself.
> I can feel his love as if he were standing,
> his hands in his pockets, watching me.
> His smile rests on the summer air,
> into the slow night darkness.
>
> Sometimes I think about the hours
> of his last morning,
> hours so immense with solitude
> I keep leaning into them
> as against a tree
> being uprooted over and over again.[4]

Mourning is an act of love, and love has the power to root you where you are. But the loved one has gone, like a stretch of land that has subsided under the sea, like that house somewhere near Johannesburg that disappeared overnight into the sheer-sided black mouth of a sinkhole with its sleeping family, leaving behind only the children's toys in the backyard. Love remains but love's territory, the land of live relationship, has been taken.

The mind sets off, footloose as a **nomad***, *wandering out across the wasteland of absence, the outgrowths of memory, the old haunts, the best times, the secrets, the emotion buried like a dog's bone below the surface of everyday life just waiting to be dug up.*

But the state of inner burning can't last, and the world goes on turning. Mourning takes four seasons, says Jewish lore. Then the living are called back amongst the living, though the dead do not disappear from their minds. Our daughter comes home from school and tells us she spent all break crying alone under a tree for her

[4] Nina Bogin, *The Winter Orchards*, p.22

grandfather. Quite a lot later, our son tells me he finds it funny that my father died in his pyjamas. Funny about the pyjamas, he says, not funny that he died.

Death is woven back into the clothing of life, stretching it, altering it, a dark thread of a new texture among the brilliant threads, so that the living wear it differently. The game of life goes on, but there is a different order of play, because with grandparents gone, parents are of the next generation to go.

If my memory of my father was as his son, it is also now more than ever as a father who will pass his memory on.

Stories in the dark

Tell me a story about when you were young, asks my son.
Bedtime becomes a carnival of the past, teeming
with tales of marbles, silkworms, soccer, dogfights,
the figure of a Zulu watchman flinging his knobkerrie
at the legs of the girl I loved
while we were out slogan-painting in the night.

A six-year old fills himself with my memory,
and his mother's memory, from yet another country,
and falls asleep here, just outside Paris, France.
We tell him our stories in English,
but he takes them with him in French,
the first language of his wilful heart.

Our children are our centre of gravity here,
the root of our immigrant tree.
We are the seed and sustenance, while they
hunger downward into French earth,
rise for the moment into a French sky,
though all this could change later:

they too could find themselves with families
whose language is a little, if not altogether strange
to their ears. My parents did not speak
their parents' mother tongue to us; my mother puzzles
when our children speak their daily French,
and they in turn could find themselves in a place

where the maps that once worked are suddenly useless,
where the simplest gestures, a dish of food or bar of song,
new words for bread, and love, and house, all contain
estrangement. Tell me a story, asks my son, in French.
I go digging back into my memories, in English,
as we work out our nightly equation of loss and gain.

JE ME SOUVIENS (2001, obsession)

One evening in February 2001, I was in a bookshop in the old Paris quarter of the Marais, at a French poetry reading given by a friend. It was not a very good reading, and my mind started wandering. For no apparent reason, I decided that I had to buy myself a copy of *Je me souviens.*

I started looking through it on the metro going home, and continued in bed. Within the next few days I found that it had gone entirely to my head. I had to finish the book, but at the same time memories of my own started rushing at me thick and fast.

One of the first of them came out of the 1960's, and concerned, not surprisingly in retrospect, an emigrant experience: the arrival by fishing boat, somewhere on the shores of South Africa, of Portuguese inhabitants evacuated from the island of Tristan da Cunha after a volcanic eruption.

I found that I had to write these memories down, but they seemed to be limitless. There was a constant mob of them, jostling at the doorway to my mind. In a matter of days, every element of the world that surrounded me became a potential repository of some association with South Africa as I had once known it.

My memory was like a tree that had been shaken by some great disturbance, and the sky was filled with wheeling birds.

A chance flash of sunlight from a windowpane and I was reminded of how we would purposefully deflect spots of sunlight around a classroom using our wristwatches. A student of mine mentioned a trip to Belize, did I know that it used to be called British Honduras? Instead of thinking about geography, I was suddenly back in Johannesburg at the age of twelve, looking at stamps from countries which existed nowhere but in my stamp album: Aden, Sierra Leone, British Honduras.

I was continuously caught within the pulsing circuits of association, engaged in a game I had become addicted to and needed to play over and over at any hour of the day or night.

By its repetitive, open-ended structure, Perec's *Je me souviens* suggested how this game might be played. What had originally irritated me about the brevity of his notation, the way he did not dwell but rather darted from the surface of one memory to the next, now seemed an ideal way to mark out, in pointillist fashion, and ultimately in book form,[5] the tiny, inter-meshed, resurfacing co-ordinates of a gone world.

JE ME SOUVIENS (souvenirs?)

The elements recorded by Perec in *Je me souviens* are generally so impersonal that they might not qualify as "memories" at all. Instead, they are the briefest of reminders, mnemonics, keys by which to re-enter a world once shared by many people at the same time.

Here, thanks to Roland Brasseur's book *Je me souviens de 'Je me souviens'* ("I Remember 'I Remember' "), which annotates the 479 references in Perec's text, is a general breakdown of its subject matter:

Cinema, music, theatre, ballet, art, dance clubs, radio programmes	163
Sport, games, exploration, scouts	49
The city of Paris, shops, buildings, transport	35

[5] Denis Hirson, *I Remember King Kong (the Boxer)*

History, politics	35
Reading, books, literature	31
School life	25
The media	24
Language, language games	22
General knowledge of war, the army, the navy	20
Health, food, cigarettes	20
Advertising	16
Diverse news items	15
Fashion, clothing, jewellery	13
Personal	11
	479

More than three hundred of Perec's items concern the world of culture, entertainment and sport, health, advertising and the media, or the urban fabric of the city of Paris. Another eighty or so involve school life, literature and language games. Less than this number concern history, politics, general knowledge of war (for the most part concerning famous military leaders and battles) and diverse news items.

As for Perec's own personal memories, they seem to barely feature at all. Those I have classified as such all have a personal slant, but are hardly intimate, or at least appear not to be. Their content includes, for example, the very long cigarette which Perec's cousin once brought home,[6] or the moment when he learnt that "Georges" meant "worker of the land".[7]

On the face of it, then, virtually all the elements in *Je me souviens* form part of the lighter collective mental souvenirs of a whole generation. The spotlight is on the convivial and inconsequential side of daily life, the city in which it is being lived, the linguistic playfulness of its inhabitants. This is Perec's intention. On the back cover of *Je me souviens* he writes:

> These… are not exactly memories, and above all not personal memories, but little pieces of the everyday, things which, in one year or another, all people of the same age saw, lived through, shared, and which then disappeared, were forgotten.

[6] *Je me souviens*, p.24

[7] p.45

What he is interested in here, he goes on to say, was not worth memorising, and could lay no claim to being part of History. But though quintessentially banal, it might nonetheless have a slightly more than banal effect when remembered, "giving rise for a few seconds to a small, impalpable feeling of nostalgia".[8]

On closer inspection these comments are deceptive, perhaps even purposefully so. Some items in the book refer to events which are far from banal, such as the capitulation of Japan,[9] or the Biafra war.[10] Others might be calculated to leave the French reader uneasy, in a country where people are prone to forgetting their own troubled recent past, such as "I remember the 121" (signatories of the declaration of the right to insubordination in the Algerian War).[11]

More intriguing, in a book which appears to be so little concerned with personal memory, are items such as "I remember the Finaly affair",[12] concerning the fate of two brothers whose parents died in deportation, and who were fought over by Catholic priests and an Israeli aunt.[13] This is one of several examples of elements which do touch in a sometimes important – but almost always inexplicit – way on aspects of Perec's own life.

In fact, throughout Perec's œuvre there are more or less deeply buried elements which might, or might not, refer to elements of his own life. The irresistible temptation to find such connections, not least of all because of their elaborate hiding places, as well as the network of meaning which they promise to reveal, has set in frenzied motion a vast and intrepid pack of literary bloodhounds. I cannot claim to have stood back indifferently from their chase.

JE ME SOUVIENS (1946-1961)

In a post-script to *Je me souviens* , Perec mentions that most of the memories recorded there relate to the period from 1946 to 1961, that is from his tenth to his twenty-fifth year.[14]

---

[8] *Je me souviens*, back cover

[9] p.22

[10] p.50

[11] p.65

[12] p.66

[13] Roland Brasseur, *Je me souviens de Je me souviens*, pp.154, 155

[14] *Je me souviens*, p.119

It is not difficult to understand why he chooses 1961 as a cut-off point. This was the year when he left France for Sfax, Tunisia, with his wife; a time when, according to her, their existence, far from the comforts of Paris, was pared down to the point of deprivation in the isolated provinces.[15] Not long after their return to Paris, Georges Perec set out in earnest to become a writer, beginning with his first major work, *Les choses* (Things), first published in 1965.

1946, on the other hand, is a far more problematic year to have chosen. Since *Je me souviens* includes few, if any, memories dating back further than this, Perec, born in 1936, has excluded virtually all reference to the first ten years of his life.

It was during this period that tragedy struck his family. The year after Perec's birth, his parents had a daughter who survived only a few weeks before dying of a malformation of the stomach. In 1940, just a week before the armistice, Perec's father, a Polish Jewish immigrant, was killed while fighting for the French Foreign Legion against the Germans.

Less than three years later his mother was interned at Drancy and then deported, probably to Auschwitz. He never saw her again. His mother's sister and both his grandfathers were also deported. He spent most of the war years in the "free zone", in a children's home and then a Catholic boarding school in Villard-de-Lans, followed by a second children's home in Lans-en-Vercors. He was adopted by his father's sister and her husband, and, in 1945, returned to Paris to live with them.[16]

1946 was the beginning of a very different kind of life for him. Referring to events from before this time in *Je me souviens* would have meant crossing back over into a deeply traumatic zone of experience, the memory of which would hardly give rise to "a small, impalpable feeling of nostalgia". Nor, of course, would it be widely shared by the members of Perec's generation

W

During the same period that he was assembling the material for *Je me souviens*, Perec completed another book, *W ou le souvenir*

[15] Paulette Perec, "Chronique de la vie de Georges Perec" in Paulette Perec (ed.), *Portrait(s) de Georges Perec*, p.58

[16] pp.13-30

d'enfance (W or the Memory of Childhood, referred to here as *W*), which he sees as not exactly parallel but akin to it.[17] Half of this book is fictional. The other half is autobiographical, a record of Perec's struggle to take possession of his own story before 1946, wresting it both from the annihilation which threatened his family, and the (purposeful or otherwise) unreliability of his own memory once he had finally overcome his desire to forget.

The second chapter of *W* begins with the statement "I have no memories of childhood".[18] This is not simply a manner of speaking. Perec, though said to have had a prodigious memory,[19] writes:

> It remains inconceivable that I should have not one memory of rue Vilin where I must nonetheless have spent most of the seven (or six) first years of my life: I underline the words "not one", meaning not one memory of place, not one memory of any face.[20]

If he has entirely forgotten the rue Vilin period, then his memories of the war years, up until 1945, are often uncertain, clouded over by the events of the times. In the wake of wider disaster he felt for a long time dispossessed of his own story. No one could question him on this because, as he writes in *W*,

> It wasn't part of my syllabus. I had been given an exemption: another story, the Big One, History with its great axe had already replied in my place: the war, the camps.[21]

When he does try to recall events such as the (probable, but in his case unconfirmed) obligation to wear the yellow star, the memories are so painful that he finds he has done mental surgery on himself to render them benign. And when referring to his life in the "free zone", where he was sent in 1942, he writes as if he has been affected by a form of partial **amnesia***. There are things he remembers, but each memory is cut off from the next

---

[17] Georges Perec, *Je suis né*, pp.83, 84

[18] p.17

[19] David Bellos, *Une vie dans les mots*, p.443

[20] quoted in Paulette Perec, "Chronique de la vie de Georges Perec", in Paulette Perec (ed.), *Portrait(s) de Georges Perec*, p.14

[21] *W ou le souvenir d'enfance*, p.17. Pun: "l'Histoire avec sa grande hache", History with its great axe, also suggests "l'Histoire avec un grand H", History with a capital H

> like that handwriting which is not cursive but made of isolated letters incapable of soldering themselves together to make a word, and which was mine until the age of seventeen or eighteen.[22]

He is in a state apart, with no point of reference; the memories he does have before returning to Paris are "pieces of life torn away from the void".[23] Yet in *W* he is also able to see that this void, created above all by the disappearance of his parents, lies at the heart of his being,[24] and his enterprise as a writer:

> I write because we lived together, because I was one amongst them, shadow in the midst of their shadows, body close to their bodies; I write because they left within me the indelible mark whose trace is writing: their memory is dead to writing; writing is the memory of their death and the affirmation of my life.[25]

In *Je me souviens*, this central absence, and everything associated with it, is precisely what goes unmentioned.

I REMEMBER v. JE ME SOUVIENS

Perec's idea for a book of sentences, or groups of sentences, beginning with the words "I remember", comes from the American Joe Brainard, who published several books based on the same principle, the first of them in 1970.

Brainard's approach could hardly have been more different from Perec's. What interests him more than anything else is his own personal world, his trials and tribulations, misconceptions and emotions, particularly concerning the question of sex, and even more particularly sex with boys and men.

In the collected *I Remember* book, more than a quarter of the entries on the first twenty pages alone are devoted to Brainard and sex, and these are the longest, one of them taking up almost a page. Entries on this topic punctuate and spill over into the rest of the book, filled as they are with the pulsing, joke-packed energies of transgression:

22 *W ou le souvenir d'enfance*, p. 97
23 p.98
24 p.26
25 pp.63, 64

> I remember "French kissing" and figuring out that it must have something to do with the tongue since there isn't anything else in the mouth except teeth.
>
> I remember that shaking or holding hands with a girl while you scratched her palm with your middle finger was somehow "dirty." (Often done as a joke and the girl would turn red and scream.)
>
> I remember in Boston a Puerto Rican boy who worked behind a glass counter in a cafetaria and his arms up to his rolled up sleeves: thick and gold and hairless.
>
> I remember early sexual experiences and rubbery knees. I'm sure sex is better now but I do miss rubbery knees.[26]

Brainard's *I Remember* is basically a fragmented work of autobiography, a theatrically unabashed exit from the closet. This does not mean that it is disconnected from collective experience. As Brainard himself put it, "I [...] feel that it is about everybody else as much as it is about me [...] I mean, I feel like I am everybody".[27] But there is still the strong impression that when he writes "I remember", the accent is on the "I", slender, vulnerable and highly personal.

This is precisely the kind of approach that Perec shunned. He too might be writing from out of a past of exclusion, as a Jewish refugee. But his texts are filled with a French sense of "pudeur", coupled with a very personal distaste for the written expression of his inner feelings. "The problems of my own interior state leave me a little cold", he wrote to Maurice Nadeau in 1969,[28] elsewhere declaring his admiration for Flaubert's "passionate coldness".[29]

Perec broke from this general line in texts such as *W*, but when it came to writing *Je me souviens*, it seems that the last person he was thinking of was himself. In fact, he invited others to contribute to his project. Marie Chaix describes a few "soirées joyeuses" shared by a group of friends during which sentences all beginning "Je me souviens" came streaming out. Perec then went through a strict sorting process before deciding on what could be used.

---

[26] Joe Brainard, *I Remember*, p.106

[27] Ron Padgett, Afterword to Brainard's *I Remember*, p.171

[28] Georges Perec, *Je suis né*, p.56

[29] Marcel Bénabou and Bruno Marcenac, "Le bonheur est un processus… on ne peut pas s'arrêter d'être heureux", in Bertelli and Ribière (eds.), *Georges Perec, entretiens et conferences,* Vol.1, 1965-1978, p.48

Chaix also mentions that Perec had not actually read but only heard of Brainard's book when he began his own.[30] When he did finally read it, he was a little disappointed, having been under the false impression "that Joe had worked like him on the collective memory".[31]

Not, as I have already pointed out, that this stopped Perec from squirreling seemingly anodyne elements into the text which are in fact emotionally charged for him. Here are a few more examples. Item 133 reads "I remember that my first bicycle had solid tyres".[32] "I still retain the physical sensation of it", Perec commented later, while acknowledging that the reference seems neutral.[33]

Even more telling is item 421, "I remember lead soldiers really made of lead, and soldiers made of clay".[34] At the age of three or four, Perec mentions in *W*, "the love that I bore for my father was expressed through a ferocious passion for lead soldiers".[35] He goes on to describe how, in the post-war years, his aunt once refused to buy him lead soldiers as a present. Later, he saved the money she gave him for the metro, only to find that he could afford nothing but clay soldiers.

But, however many personal allusions are hidden in the text, it contains a powerful element of self-abnegation. Significantly, the reference in *Je me souviens* to the "Vel d'Hiv", a Paris velodrome, concerns the sport of cycling,[36] whereas at the same infamous spot some 13,000 Jews were rounded up for deportation in 1942. This must, of course, have been a conscious choice on Perec's part, perhaps even one laced with irony. In an interview, he himself points to the Vel d'Hiv as the place where the worlds of sport and the concentration camp overlapped for the first time, a theme central to the fictional half of *W*.[37]

Looked at as a whole, if "Je me souviens" is Perec's rite of integration into the normality of post-war France, then it pays a price for this act. It is not only a book of memory, but also, in ways which are central to Perec's own story, a book of forgetting.

---

30 Marie Chaix, Preface to Brainard, *I Remember (Je me souviens)*, p.8

31 Monique Pétillon, "Ce qui ce passe quand il ne se passe rien" in Bertelli and Ribière (eds), *Georges Perec, entretiens et conférences*, Vol.1, 1965-1978, p.215

32 *Je me souviens*, p.41

33 *Je suis né*, p.84

34 p.103

35 *W ou le souvenir d'enfance*, p.48

36 *Je me souviens*, p.49

37 Patrice Fardeau, "En dialogue avec l'époque" in Bertelli and Ribière (eds), *Georges Perec, entretiens et conférences*, Vol.2, 1979-1981, p.60

In *W*, where Perec does allow himself to write of Jewishness and its mortal consequence, he records a memory involving precisely that explosive combination of the personal and the historical which is missing from *Je me souviens*:

> I remember photos showing the walls of the ovens lacerated by the fingernails of those who were gassed and a chess-game made of balls of bread.[38]

In contrast, *Je me souviens* appears to be almost impossibly light. And yet, given the way its fragments are formulated, could it not retain a distant echo of the writing that came out of the concentration camps?

In narratives of that time, the individual is seen to be crushed by the levelling pressures of constantly depersonalising, life-threatening degradation. As a result, the textual meaning of the first person singular is itself altered. Though still used, it loses its individual substance: "The depth of 'I' continues to exist, but no longer refers to any subject" says Luba Jurgenson in her study of this writing that came out of the camps.[39]

Jurgenson goes on to describe how, in the camps, the self is sunk in collective life, which is in turn experienced as "a supreme degree of dispossession".[40] Here, in this vein, are the Athletes in the fictional section of *W*:

> You should see these tarred and feathered wrestlers, these long-distance runners hopping or crawling around, you should see those who have survived the marathon, limping, frozen to the bone, trotting between two tight-knit rows of sideline Judges armed with rods and bludgeons, you should see them, these skeletal Athletes with their sallow faces, spines constantly bent, bare skulls gleaming, eyes filled with panic, sores oozing pus, all these indelible marks of endless humiliation, bottomless terror, all these proofs administered each hour, each day, each second, of a conscious, organized, hierarchical crushing, you should see this great machine at work, each cog adding with implacable efficacy to the systematic annihilation of men [...][41]

[38] *W or the Memory of Childhood*, p. 215
[39] *L'expérience concentrationnaire est-elle indicible?*, p.73
[40] p.83
[41] *W or the Memory of Childhood*, pp.219,220

Is it possible that for all the descriptive lightness of "Je me souviens", it still bears a deep trace of this reality? Perec's use of the first person singular, "je", is after all ostensibly a front for the representative, shared "nous", the "we" that had to be painstakingly pieced together after the wartime experience.

RE-MEMBERING (1)

I am still trying to understand why Perec's *Je me souviens* should have had such a potent effect on me. I suppose there must be several reasons for this; the first is perhaps revealed in the way I started compulsively remembering South Africa in the wake of mourning for my father.

The bond between us had been an integral part of my bond with the country; my sense of involvement in place was linked to his. When he was arrested, this sense paradoxically deepened.

I was drawn into a dark maze where the corridors of prison became extension of the corridors that his absence bored into me, while the world of political outcasts Inside seemed echo my own feeling of being an outsider. The wound of his uprooting from our lives had raw edges to it which were both personal and political. The submerged anger I felt towards him, the pain and helplessness were inevitably muted by the meaning of his actions in South Africa at that time.

I do not take the image of the wound to be negative, but central as a well to my being. As Edmond Jabès says somewhere, "Each wound is a source", and the source, both personal and in terms of place, seems to deepen in retrospect.

I think my memories surfaced after my father died not only in my desire to remember him, but also because something of the bond between myself and South Africa had been shaken. Perhaps it is the corresponding seismograph that became visible to me while reading *Je me souviens.*

Then, on a different level, there is the relationship between this book and the act of remembering itself.

Here are four statements about the act of remembering.

The first is that this act involves many past events which have become immobilized in the mind. The more these events have been spoken of, written of, mulled over, returned to, firmly slotted into the story of oneself, the story of a place and time, the less likely it is that their basic contours will alter. They may be edited with the passage of time, utterly eroded through forgetting. But before that, whatever their truth, and even if their content is challenged, they have a tendency to become anecdotes, locked up in the long-term parking zone of the self, only shifting under unusual circumstances.

Harry Mathews, who wrote a beautifully moving elegy to Georges Perec using the same form as *Je me souviens*, includes the following "I remember" in his book:

> I remember that of all the forms imagination can take, memory is usually the most inert.[42]

The second statement about the act of remembering is that it occurs at contradictory speeds. At one extreme it involves sprinting from one memory to the next, following a sequence as unpredictable as it is elliptical, along a many-centred series of paths, zigzagging between different subjects, time-periods, perspectives, widening in scope by invisible association, sometimes revealing what is being remembered from several angles at once. Memory has definite cubist tendencies. Or, as Virginia Woolf writes, memory is a seamstress who "runs her needle in and out, up and down, hither and thither".[43]

At the other extreme, when remembering, one might dwell for long periods on a single memory, isolating it, blowing it up beyond all proportion, refusing to move on from the sadness of it or sunbathing in its heat. As Susan Sontag puts it, establishing a parallel with the nature of photography, "memory freeze-frames".[44]

The third statement is this: something special happens when, after a long time, one remembers a seemingly banal object or phrase or experience, that has been lost for ages under the thickly packed archaeological layers of experience. This is something too small to be part of a Significant Story. As a result, its nature has not been blunted, shaped and reshaped by the repetitive habits

---

[42] *The Orchard*, p.23

[43] quoted by Steven Rose, *The Making of Memory*, p.319

[44] *Regarding the Pain of Others*, p.22

of the mind, slotted into the economical form of an anecdote. Neglected, unnoticed, it has been shielded from the dust and acids of time.

As a result, such items are strangely, disproportionately alive when dug up, "miraculously torn away from their insignificance" says Perec.[45] And this is not only because of the sudden flash of recognition which greets them, but because whole contexts come to light in their company, illuminated by the filament of newness which burns in them for a brief moment.

By mentioning so many of these items in *Je me souviens,* Perec is, in a way, making a statement against the potential inertia of memory. There is no time to delve as in *W,* but rather the relief of the skater in constant movement, pausing perhaps but then curving on from one discovery to the next with the rhythmic pulse of the free-associating mind. To this extent, the book reflects the syntax of memory itself, even more so given the way Perec has worked on the surface pattern of his text, compacting each item to more or less the same size and then numbering it.

If Perec's text were read aloud, it could in its cumulative regularity come to sound like a litany or mantric invocation, transcending the great diversity of its content to enter a different order of time. This might explain the state Perec says he was in while writing his text, one "of suspension [...] something of the order of meditation".[46]

The last statement about the act of remembering is that it becomes particularly intense at times of great personal change, when the field of memory shudders with turbulence, as if hit by a fierce wind, or fire, or a river in flood. There is a sudden rush of things to remember, markers of the past uprooted and thrown together in unexpected ways in the flux of the moment. The result is that there seems to be a reordering of time, a "re-membering" as Stephen Rose puts it in a different context.[47]

This is perhaps the central reason why the rhythmic structure but dispersed content of *Je me souviens* reached into me so strongly after my father's death. I was in the process of letting go after more than a year's mourning; in creating a mobile, elastic surface

---

[45] *Je me souviens*, back cover

[46] Georges Perec, *Je suis né*, p.89

[47] *The Making of Memory*, p.104

by leaping unpredictably from one item of memory to the next, Perec's book works at the speed of release.

When taxed by readers about the inaccuracy of some of his entries (and Roland Brasseur finds "almost 70 clear errors or blanks"),[48] Perec replies: "my memory is intact. It is perhaps false, but it is intact".[49] He also speaks of "the paroxysm of real life which submerges and continually destroys the work of putting things in order."[50] What interests him, then, is the act of remembering as a vulnerable, mortal process, erratic and open-ended.

The last sentence of Perec's book reads "Je me souviens", with no full stop. At the bottom of the page is written "*(à suivre)*", (to be continued).[51] This is followed, at Perec's request, by several blank pages for the reader's own use. I can imagine them being filled many times over. By the time one has read (or written) 480 sentences beginning "Je me souviens", or "I remember", the first person singular might have dissolved in the act of remembering, which goes on irresistably flowing as if by itself.

I REMEMBER (Paris, circa 1975-1980)

I remember how soft French men's voices seemed to me, even if their faces were strong. And how surprised I was to find that their handshake was almost never a crunching attempt at domination.

I remember trying to get cheek-kissing right, never knowing how many kisses were expected, colliding with the other person's nose, and learning to master the dry kiss.

I remember how sore my mouth muscles were after trying to get the narrow French vowel sounds right.

I remember a friend of mine in a Vietnamese restaurant at Jussieu helping the waiter to write a love letter in French.

---

[48] Roland Brasseur, *Je me souviens de Je me souviens*, pp.271-273

[49] Philippe Carle and Francis Marmande, "Georges Perec: 'Je me souviens du jazz'", in Bertelli and Ribière (eds.), *Georges Perec, entretiens et conférences*, Vol.2, 1979-1981, p.41

[50] *Je suis né*, p.91

[51] *Je me souviens*, p. 116

I remember the thick black lines of defaced May 1968 graffiti high up on the walls of Jussieu University.

I remember "Je t'aime bien Lili, Je t'aime bien au lit aussi", and Folon's poster of a man rowing across the sea in a pair of woman's lips.

I remember Alain Suchon's song "Allô maman bobo", over and over on the radio.

I remember the vague shock at the musical mix on some radio stations: a bit of Nana Mouskouri, and then a bit of Bach, followed by Maxime le Forestier, or Idir, or Léo Ferré. Also, the way a female radio announcer's voice could sound like a stocking being slowly peeled away from a shapely leg.

I remember Bernard Hinault's nickname, "le Blaireau".

I remember when Yannick Noah had short hair.

I remember trying to understand how Simone de Beauvoir could possibly say "vous" to Sartre.

I remember wondering how people could talk so much while they were having a meal.

I remember a poster in the metro announcing that for the sake of one's health one should not drink more than a litre of wine a day.

I remember when you could get a deposit for wine bottles that had little stars moulded in the glass just above the base.

I remember a poster for Boursin: "Du vin, du pain, du Boursin", with a picture of a glass of wine and a baguette with a knot in it reminding you not to forget the cheese.

I remember the graffiti in the metro, "Un Kroissant contre Empain", and the sense of doom surrounding the news of Baader and Meinhof's imprisonment.

I remember the rattling old metros with varnished wooden seats. First-class metro carriages. The sound of crickets that were hidden somewhere in the rubble among the rails. And "DUBO, DUBON, DUBONNET" painted against a white background in the tunnel.

I remember how much smoking there used to be in public places.

I remember the scandal surrounding Giscard d'Estaing's "sniffer planes".

I remember Giscard d'Estaing on television announcing to the French nation that he hoped everyone would have a good summer holiday.

I remember that I had never felt so unprotected in a motorcar as when driving in an old 2CV.

I remember when meter maids were called "aubergines".

I remember the women all dressed in black as if they were in mourning, selling wine and pain poilane sandwiches at "La Tartine".

I remember when Paris tap-water was nick-named "Château Chirac".

I remember seeing some Boat People walking barefoot in the middle of winter outside a hostel in the suburbs of Paris. French girls in neat little tutus doing some ballet for them. And then, in reply, thin Vietnamese women up on the stage dressed in black, arms raised, bending as if their dance was a forest in a storm.

I remember a May Day parade with black dustbin-men near the front, beating out a rhythm on the upturned metal bins strapped to their bodies.

I remember soldiers collecting rubbish in the streets after the dustmen's strike. Unsightly heaps of muck against the perfect facades. The rising stench in the heat.

I remember Women's Liberation groups in May Day parades, the *Histoires d'Elles* magazine, and the slogan about a man being as necessary to a woman as a bicycle was to a fish.

I remember how strange it was to see women making themselves up in public, especially while in the metro, examining themselves in a hand-mirror and laying on lipstick or powdering their cheeks, then gazing at the result, as if they were all alone.

I remember when lots of young women washed their hair in henna. And lots of young men sat around at parties and in other places playing the darbouka.

I remember Allen Ginsberg at the American Center on Boulevard Raspail, squeezing a harmonium while chanting a William Blake poem. And then Peter Orlovsky reading a poem about making love with a woman, and getting a lot of laughs.

I remember a workman blowing a warning signal on a bright brass horn, on the railway tracks just outside the Gare du Nord.

I remember the slight unreality of the fact that Peter Brook should have a theatre just above the Gare du Nord, behind a façade on the corner of a Paris street. Then entering to see the magic that was going on in there.

I remember the film of Ariane Mnouchkine's *1789,* with actors explaining in urgent, breathless words what they had witnessed during the French revolution.

I remember that I was preparing material for a street parade in Le Havre when the news came over the radio about schoolchildren being shot in the streets of Soweto.

I remember reading *Le Monde* over someone's shoulder in the metro, and discovering that Rick Turner had been assassinated.

I remember the shop-front synagogues on the rue des Ecouffes and the rue des Rosiers, and the sepia feeling of walking back through my own past.

I remember glimpsing Georges Perec at a film festival, where the *Ellis Island* documentary he had made with Robert Bober was being shown.

I remember that all over Paris you could find a place to buy a fat Tunisian sandwich: tuna, hard boiled egg, lettuce and olive oil, black olives and potato, with or without harissa.

I remember when almost everyone I knew lived in a chambre de bonne, with a single Turkish latrine shared by all the residents of the top floor.

I remember trying to learn how to flush a Turkish latrine and then escape without getting wet.

I remember when a glazier or knife-sharpener would sometimes come shouting down the street.

I remember how often there would be accordion players, or organ grinders, or a New Orleans brass band at the market place, or elsewhere out in the streets of one neighbourhood or another. A young woman with hennaed hair and mascara singing Piaf or *Mac the Knife*. Trestle tables set out in the street and people sharing a meal.

I remember when a man came to the door selling carpets. I bought one with a pattern of birds against a burnt sienna background, and felt as if I had finally arrived.

I remember a woman lying on her back on that carpet in the full spring sunlight.

I remember when there was a Paris telephone directory that supplied everyone's telephone number street by street and building by building.

I remember the joke about the man from Marseilles who was told that if you wanted to use the public telephone you had to put the coins in the slot and then dial with one hand, and hold the receiver in the other. He wanted to know which hand you talked with.

I remember late night queues outside broken public telephones from which you could make long distance calls for free. I called my family in London, feeling as excited as a thief.

RE-MEMBERING (2)

In September 2003, Sami Frey's performance of *Je me souviens* returned to Paris for a three-month stint. The smart old Théâtre de la Madeleine was packed out when I went with three French friends. There was Frey, over seventy years old, dapper and beautifully groomed, pedalling – apparently just as he had fifteen years ago – on a bicycle which swivelled though its spinning wheels did not move forward. He travelled meditatively, sometimes desperately, his headlight at one point directed into near darkness, always getting nowhere, while an over-elaborate decor of cloth arranged in peaks almost imperceptibly rose and fell around him. There was his breathing pattern as he worked at the pedals. There was his eloquent, melodious voice.

The audience was highly attentive, and responsive. I hadn't expected the text to provoke so much *laughter.* Nor had I realized how many songs were hidden within Perec's lines.

A few weeks before the performance, I dreamed that a portly, unshaven man, resembling a student of mine, stood on a ridge of land which formed part of the French national border, reciting items from Perec's *Je me souviens.*

> To describe space: name it, trace it, like those makers of sea-charts who saturated the coastlines with names of ports, names of capes, names of creeks, until in the end the earth was separated from the sea by no more than a continuous ribbon of text.[52]

I imagine myself as the man in my dream, standing at the French border, reciting Perec's text which knows no intrinsic borders: in the blink of an eye memory veers from the routes of one time and place to those of another. The living and the dead, creatures of fiction or flesh and blood, stones, stars, oceans, moments of love, anger, despair, a falling leaf, a bird in a dream, whole landscapes, toothache, sweet-wrappers, a flea on the inside of a sock, hotels, cuckoo-clocks, anything from out of the past can escape being forgotten, and find a new place in the constantly altering flux of the present.

The world of childhood in a distant country is less than a split second away from the city where the immigrant makes another home, and which in turn soon fills with memories of its own. But these memories nonetheless appear less rooted than the old ones, lighter though they may be dark, strange with the strangeness of the new place itself. For the immigrant, memory of this new place becomes a kind of invention, like the act of writing itself.

[52] Georges Perec, *Espèces d'espaces*, p.26

Banality (1)

Georges Perec is particularly interested in banality, in what he calls the "infra-ordinary" contours of the everyday world:

> What occurs each day and returns each day, the banal, the everyday, the obvious, the common, the ordinary, the infra-ordinary, the back- ground noise, the habitual: how does one give an account of it, examine it, describe it?[53]

Convinced that our senses have been dulled by a cocktail of habit and spectacular media news, he wants to hunt down those things which are "common to all" (the original etymological sense of the word 'banal') and might speak to us of our own condition.

He minutely describes various surfaces of the material world around him, item by item, using unembellished language to establish a precise record of the surface he has chosen, apparently devoid of subjectivity or emotion. "Oblige yourself to see more flatly", he instructs himself.[54]

The resulting text sometimes reads like a kind of exercise. For example, he draws up an inventory of all the objects to be found on his desk. But since he is in the process of writing at this desk, his text is also included in the inventory, and is duly rewritten a second time, but in slightly altered form, as if it had been corrected in the meanwhile.[55]

Here, Perec traces and so conserves a surface at a given moment in time, but also records the inevitable changes in this surface, even at the time of writing. By admitting the tenuousness of words before the constant alteration of the world, he ultimately lays his writing bare to the process of mortality.

This double concern becomes even clearer in a text where Perec reaches through the surface he is describing to touch on his own history. In 1974, he set out a fairly elaborate and never entirely completed plan to visit at various times, over a period of twelve years, twelve places in Paris with particular significance to him, and draw up an inventory of what he found there.[56]

---

53 *L'infra-ordinaire, p.11*

54 *Espèces d'espaces, p.101*

55 *L'infra-ordinaire*, pp. 107-119

56 *Espèces d'espaces*, pp.108-110

One of these places was rue Vilin, where he spent the first six or seven years of his life. Here is the beginning of his first description of this street:

> Thursday 27th February 1969,
> about 4p.m.
>
> Rue Vilin begins at 29 rue de Couronnes, opposite some new buildings, recent high-rises which already have something old about them.
> On the right (even numbers), a three-sided building: one facade overlooking rue Vilin, another overlooking the rue des Couronnes, the third, narrow one, describing the sharp angle between these two streets; at street level, a café-restaurant whose sky-blue front is trimmed with yellow.
> On the left (odd numbers), no.1 has recently been given a face-lift.[57]

In the middle of this record, Perec finds himself

> At number 24 (this is the house where I lived):
> Firstly a single-storied building, with, on the ground floor, a door (boarded up); all around, old traces of paint and above, not yet altogether obliterated, the sign
>
> WOMEN'S HAIRDRESSER'S
>
> Then a low building with a door giving onto a long paved courtyard with a few irregularities (stairways of two or three steps). To the right, a long single-storied building (once giving onto the road by way of the boarded-up door of the hairdressing salon) with two concrete steps leading up to it (it is in this building that we lived; the hairdressing saloon was my mother's).
> At the back, a formless building. To the left, rabbit hutches of some sort. I did not go in.[58]

There are six descriptions of rue Vilin. They bear witness to the deterioration, and the beginning of the demolition, of a street which has today almost entirely disappeared. They also record

---

[57] *L'infra-ordinaire*, pp.15-16
[58] pp.18-19

the remaining traces of Perec's brief life with his parents. This double devastation is recorded by way of the most banal detail, using language which has been stripped to a bare minimum, apparently devoid of subjectivity, but fitted with an emotional depth charge.

Here is Perec's description of rue Vilin on 13th January, 1971:

> From number 36, a woman leaves: she has been living there for 36 years; she had only come for three months; she remembers the hairdresser from number 24 very well:
> - She didn't stay very long.[59]

That is all. By the next line, Perec has already passed on to numbers 41, 43 and 45. It is surely impossible that the woman's words have had no effect on him. His restraint adds tension to the description, and it is this tension which Perec seeks out, a chink in the surface where a sharp personal question can be lodged. "To look beyond this place, to find there a feeling of insecurity or transform it into a question, one must describe it with the attention of a maniac".[60]

Banal, minute description saturates the surface, until it is "so encumbered with details that it no longer exists at all".[61] This seems both an echo of Perec's personal experience of annihilation, and, ultimately, a sublime act of revenge.

Banality (2: The ordinary)

Several black South African writers have commented on the difficulties involved in creating fiction during the apartheid years. Es'kia Mphahlele refers to this reality, with its heavy polarity of good and evil, as "a crushing cliché",[62] Njabulo Ndebele names it as "mind-bogglingly spectacular",[63] far easier to merely represent than to transform in literary terms. Lewis Nkosi sees writing under these circumstances being reduced to journalism,

---

59 *L'infra-ordinaire*, pp.27,28

60 Jean Liberman, "Georges Perec et Robert Bober: 'Ellis Island, c'est le temps où les Etats-Unis incarnaient la terre promise'", in Bertelli and Ribière (eds.), *Georges Perec, entretiens et conférences*, Vol.2, 1979–1981, p.141

61 Claudette Oriol-Boyer, "Ce qui stimule ma racontouze", in Bertelli and Ribière (eds.), as above, p.176

62 *Down Second Avenue*, p.218

63 *The Rediscovery of the Ordinary*, p.41

and "the journalistic fact parading outrageously as imaginative literature".[64]

What Ndebele suggests as an antidote to the hypnotic power of the spectacular, is a return to "the ordinary lives of people" which "should be the direct focus of political interest because they constitute the *very content* of the struggle".[65]

In the fourteenth century, according to Raymond Williams, "ordinary" was a word "commonly applied to persons able to act 'in their own right', in ecclesiastical and legal affairs".[66]

"The ordinary", in these terms, refers to a latent source of power at a time of oppression, a means of going to ground, seeking regeneration in the palpable energies of the everyday. Perec turns to the same resource, feeling surrounded by destructive forces. Before him lie "the prisons of abundance, the fascinating traps of happiness" of the consumer society;[67] all around him, the media, spreading the message that life can only "be revealed through the spectacular".[68] Behind him, the devastating trail of the past.

Russia

For the propaganda machine of the apartheid regime, it went without saying that the Russians were communists, and that they and all those on their side were plotting to end what was known as "white civilization" in South Africa. In fact, the government let it be known that all its radical opponents were communists. They were everywhere, hiding under the beds.

I thought about this, imagining the shadows under the beds of our city, flecked with red. Since the government was wrong about everything in the first place, the communists might have been right. Except that there weren't any communists in our family. This my father made perfectly clear to me from an early age. So the government was not only wrong about what it was doing, but also about who we were. Or about who my father was. But the government was right that he was on the wrong side. Which was the right side (the left side). And which I was of course on, too.

---

64 "Fiction by Black South Africans" in Beier (ed.), *An Introduction to African Literature*, p.222

65 *The Rediscovery of the Ordinary* , p.57, Ndebele's italics

66 *Keywords*, p.255

67 *Les choses*, p.80

68 *L'infra-ordinaire*, p.9

My father was a Trotskyist. In the Concise Oxford Dictionary, this word is given side by side with **Trotskyite** *n. derog.* But at least the words are *there.* My American word-processor nonetheless underscores both of them with a serrated red line. There always seems to be something beyond the pale about them, whether *derog.* or not. But in the Johannesburg of the early 1960's, I knew nothing of all this.

All I knew was that, behind the locked door of our living room, in the middle of balmy weekend afternoons, my father engaged in a lot of deep secret plotting. Why should I care by what name the plotters went? If my father was among them, how could they possibly be wrong? Then, next thing, he was in prison. I understood little of the reasoning that landed him there; hardly anything, apart from the rightness.

Against the void of his absence, I pasted a series of images. There was Trotsky himself, the round ice-white lenses of his glasses and the shred of his beard, with Lenin of the pugnacious cheeks at his shoulder. Behind them shifted anonymous, bulky bodies in the vast cold squares of Moscow, strapped into greatcoats, bearing rifles fixed with bayonets. There were other bodies running. Some had fallen, their inert forms oddly bringing the scene more sharply to life. This is what a revolution looked like. Perhaps at some point in time, these images, gleaned from various books in our house, merged in my mind with images of Sharpeville.

For my father, it seemed to me, what happened in Russia in 1917 could and should happen, had already begun to happen before things started going wrong, right where we were.

This also means that, more generally, through my father, I found a link between the Russian past and the South African present. But this seemed to have nothing to do with our family history. I do not remember actually asking my father where his family was from. He had so strenuously cut himself off from his family that wherever they were from, he almost seemed to will himself to be from where we were at the time, which was South Africa. In fact, both my father's parents came from outside Riga, and where that was I only discovered years later.

Then there was my mother. She was in the background of my life, with a paleness that matched her white doctor's coat, tending like my father to the fate of others, but in a way that left her remote from me.

She did, however, occasionally give me an inkling of her family's Russian past. There was a particular memory of childhood, which she related a few times. One day when she was about seven years old, she came home from school to find her mother in the doorway, weeping helplessly, holding a letter which informed her that her father, my mother's grandfather, had been banished from his shtetl outside Minsk, to Siberia.

Recently, she described the way in which this event affected her own sense of identity:

> When I was a girl, although I was born in Palestine, and was growing up in South Africa, it seemed to me that I myself had lived in Russia; or rather that I had grown up, not in Russia, but out of Russia. My mother's past became my own past.
>
> And this idea seemed to take root at a very particular time, when my grandfather was sent into exile. There in a family photograph stood a tall, well-built, clear-eyed man. He was deeply religious, a schochet, the centre of his family and his shtetl. And because he insisted on practising his religion, he was sent to a faraway prison with no bars but surrounded by an icy emptiness.[69]

This text buzzes with revelation. In Johannesburg, my mother felt she was from elsewhere, deeply displaced, dreaming of a past (as she also dreamed of a future) outside of South Africa. She had a deep-felt sense of her own Russian history, which included her grandfather being hounded from his home by the Bolsheviks, years before he was sent to Siberia at the time of Stalin. This history was made out of her mother's stories, peopled by members of her family and others around them. And, at least in my mother's memory, it took root in her when there was a question of exile, most likely in the fertile heat of her own mother's emotion. It was an intimate history, but also one of displacement, place growing thin as a line of perspective stretched to vanishing point.

If my mother rooted herself in the wound of the past, my father transferred this process. Born in South Africa, his roots were in

[69] Yael Hirson, *A Story for Anna*, p.1

the political wounding of the present. For him, Jewishness was a burning coal that could not be held in the palm of the hand. For her, it was hidden in an egg of silence.

Would I have wanted to listen to more of her stories? Would I have wanted to plant my heart anywhere but where my feet were, on the high dolomite plateau of Johannesburg? Whatever the case, there were two dimly articulated Russias in my life. The Russia of Trotsky's unfulfilled promise which, transferred to South Africa, engulfed my father in the darkness of prison. And the Russia of my mother, a place of tragedy and uncompleted mourning for the past her mother had once torn herself from, trailing off into a silence deeper than snow.

Russia was inside me, it was where I must in some way have come from, but it was a place that I wanted no part of; a place of the dead. Only much later, when I left South Africa as an adult, met my mother's parents and listened to their stories, did Russia seem to come alive once more.

Exile

"Exile" is derived from the Latin root, *exilium*, banishment. Once upon a time, it was applied to those who had been excluded from a given place by circumstance or force, or chose to leave before force was applied, but could not choose to go back.

In apartheid South Africa, exiles were the ones who were not there but stood plotting in the wings, or took up arms, wearing the painfully earned, dark medal of exclusion.

Exiles had sharp political ideas. They belonged to political parties. They stuck together, give or take a bit of in-fighting, in foreign capitals. They pored over news from home. With more or less success they managed to dress the wounds of separation, while learning how to bide their time. Sometimes, they fell headlong through the crack between the world they lived in but rejected, and the world they wanted to live in but which rejected them:

you live as if you'd never die
because this is not where you lead your life
yet death walks in your body
death comes down the trail of your guts
death is knotted into your wings[70]

Exile meant there was an umbilical cord between you and the place where you thought what was happening was wrong. Sooner or later, you hoped to use that cord to climb back to where you came from. In South Africa, exile meant deep attachment to the politics of place.

Exile also meant that you could survive this place, which had threatened your life. You might even survive in a way that was more comfortable for you than for those who had been left behind. Of life in South Africa during the apartheid years, Oupa Thando Mthimkulu writes that "there was no worse exile than home".[71]

In *Ellis Island*, Georges Perec, thinking of his own emigrant Polish family, makes the connection between exile and survival:

designated as Jewish
and since Jewish a victim
owing life only to chance and exile[72]

In this context, the word takes on a widely sweeping meaning. It attaches to all those who have been sent off into the wilderness in the wake of repression. Men, women, children, masses with hurried bundles and blank haggard faces moving across borders in search of one more day of life. These people have not necessarily been picked out as individuals, were not always opponents of a regime, and might be on the move only because they are members of a clan or religious community, or were simply living in the wrong place at the wrong time.

"Exile" easily merges with the word "exodus".

The same word has been used to describe not a forced social movement but a state of deep inner unease, an exclusion of the body from the paradise of spiritual fulfilment. This will only be reached in death, as when one of France's twentieth century

[70] Breytenbach, "Exile, representative", *In Africa even the Flies are Happy*, tr. from the Afrikaans by Denis Hirson, p.64

[71] "Out of Africa into Exile"

[72] *Ellis Island*, p.55

saints, Saint Thérèse of Lisieux, asked whether life was sad, answered "It is exile which is sad, not life".[73]

Today, more and more frequently, "exile" has come to combine the ideas of both displacement and existential turmoil so great that return to any terrestrial starting point is excluded, and the spirit might never find a resting place. As early as 1916, in *A Portrait of the Artist as a Young Man*, James Joyce pitted himself against home, fatherland and church, "using for my defence the only arms I allow myself to use – silence, exile, and cunning".[74]

In these terms, "exile" refers to a consciously recognised, if not chosen, existential state. It has come to resemble another word, highly fashionable in the late 1960's and 70's: "alienation", referring to anything from a state of powerlessness to a sense of self-estrangement, and more generally providing "evidence of extensive feeling of a division between *man* and *society*."[75]

Exile, to the extent that it is wielded and not passively borne, nonetheless holds out a hope where alienation is moulded in despair. The person who might be called an "existential exile", like the political exile, potentially changes the dissatisfaction of this state into a source of fuel, using it to work upon the world.

But however it is forged, and whoever wields it, exile is a double-edged blade, cutting into the heart just as it might cut out a new space in the world.

Nomad (1)

What of the exile who does not adapt to new conditions, but sooner or later lets go of the old country, or was too young to know another country, or refuses its backward-leaning claim or invitation to belong? What of the one who goes on wandering, meets a partner, maybe has children, buys a house, hardly leaves the host city, yet sets out on a quest of the spirit that leads elsewhere, which becomes Elsewhere? This is one kind of nomad, mind fixed on that constantly elusive space at the edge of the present which is light and ready as a blank page, deep as the interior of the self, higher than the dark reaches of human folly.

73 Mgr. Guy Gaucher, *Sainte Thérèse de Lisieux*, p.32
74 p.247
75 Raymond Williams, *Keywords*, p.36. Williams' italics

> For nomads, the notion of past and future is perhaps subservient to the experience of elsewhere. Something that has gone, or is awaited, is hidden elsewhere in another place.[76]

Georges Perec was a person of this kind. One commentator, Paul Virilio, sees him "walking along the streets of exodus",[77] "the prototype of the 'urban nomad' ",[78] wandering along a gulf of time with the destruction of the Second World War to one side and the post-war demolition of organic urban structure to the other.

In *Espèces d'espaces*, Perec describes his love of walking aimlessly through Paris, carried along by the atmosphere of the city itself.[79] But at the end of the same book he expresses the deep sense of dispossession underlying, and undermining, his relationship to space:

> I would like there to be places which were stable, immobile, intangible, untouched and almost untouchable, immovable, rooted; places which might be references, points of departure, sources:
>
> The country of my birth, my family home, the house where I might have been born, the tree that I would have seen growing (my father having planted it on the day of my birth), the attic of my childhood filled with intact souvenirs...
>
> Such places do not exist, and it is because they do not exist that space is called into question, ceases to be taken for granted, ceases to be incorporated, ceases to be appropriated. Space is a doubt: I must ceaselessly mark it out, designate it; it is never mine, never given to me, I must make a conquest of it.[80]

Here there is no absolute place of belonging, but the constant possibility of free fall. The plug has been pulled from the surface of the past, and now no space can be taken for granted. Perec describes France, his place of birth, as "un pays natal d'adoption", a birthplace by adoption.[81] Every step of the wanderer, every word

---

[76] John Berger, "The Culture of Arrival" in *The Guardian*, 12th Oct. 2002, p.14

[77] Paul Virilio, "Un homme qui marche", in Paulette Perec (ed.), *Portrait(s) de Georges Perec*, p.159

[78] p.161

[79] *Especes d'espaces*, p.124

[80] p.179

[81] *La disparition*, p.56

of the writer crosses the border of impossibility to reach the palpable, tenuous feast of existence.

Nomad (2)

During our last two years of high-school, we had a history textbook entitled *Illustrated History for Senior Certificate*, which went by the name of one of its authors, van Jaarsveld. Less than half this book of 553 pages is devoted to "European History", conveniently omitting 1789 and instead beginning in the nineteenth century, when "revolutionary currents… dashed against the bastions of the existing order."[82]

The rest of the book sets out the history of the apartheid state, using the dead language of administrative procedure, spiked, by way of light relief, with dizzying tales of perfect heroism:

> Amid wild war cries, *Daniel Bezuidenhout* performed his heroic deed. Wounded, he jumped on a horse and went to warn the next laagers. And *Tienie Oosthuizen* will never be forgotten because of his courageous deed which saved the trapped van Rensburgs. He weaved his way through the Zulu assegais on his horse like an indestructible spirit, seized gunpowder from a waggon and saved the trapped trekkers from a certain death.[83]

The true mission of this book was to rope its young readers into the business of nation-building, raising slab by reinforced concrete slab the house of apartheid:

> All groups played a role in the building up of the country […] and have to abide by common frontiers within which their future has to be worked out by mutual co-operation so that each can fill his (sic) rightful place and contribute to the development of the whole of the Republic of South Africa.[84]

---

[82] F.A. van Jaarsveld and Theo van Wijk, *Illustrated History for Senior Certificates Stds. IX and X*, p.8

[83] F.A. van Jaarsveld and Theo van Wijk, *Illustrated History for Senior Certificates Stds. IX and X*, pp.297, 298, authors' italics

[84] p.179

And here, on the same page, is an illustration of what van Jaarsveld and van Wijk mean by "all groups", and their "rightful place":

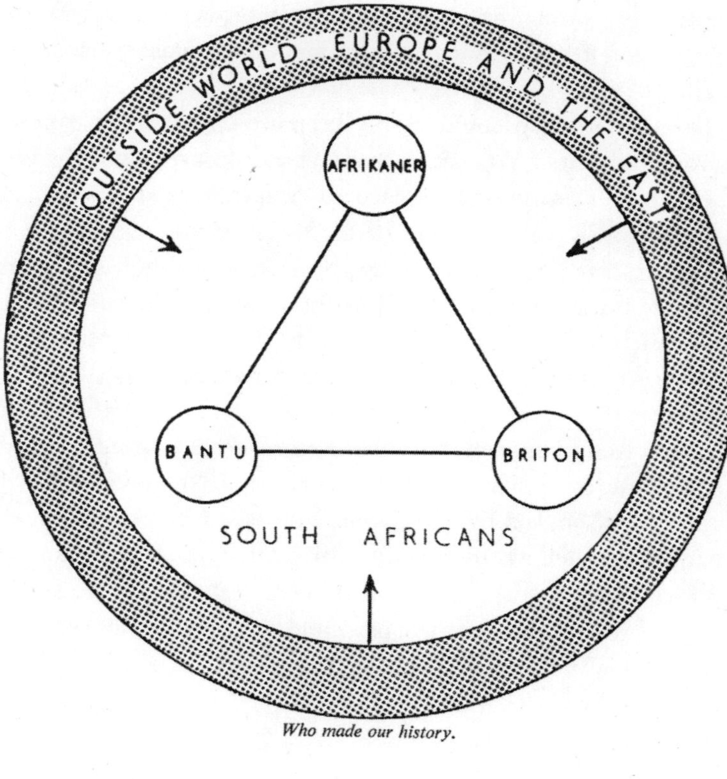

Who made our history.

There are several striking aspects to this diagram. Firstly, there is the blatant supremacy of AFRIKANER at the top of the pyramid, despite (or because of) the fact that this particular edition of the book was destined for, inter alia, the offspring of both BANTU and BRITON (which should read ENGLISH SPEAKING SOUTH AFRICAN, BRITON being a misnomer by the time this book was first published in 1961, when South Africa left the Commonwealth to become a republic).

Secondly, there is the way in which the three circumscribed groups are locked together, while being simultaneously held apart.

Thirdly, OUTSIDE WORLD EUROPE AND THE EAST appears as a moat, entirely isolating the SOUTH AFRICANS. The arrows, no doubt intended to show that AFRIKANER, BANTU and BRITON originally came from OUTSIDE WORLD, EUROPE AND THE EAST, appear instead to be exerting pressure, if not actually flying, inwards.

Last but not at all least, no specific mention is made of AFRICA at all.

The entire vision could hardly be more completely vacuum-packed and static. What it did make clear to any pupil was the fixed and incontrovertible place in South African society of AFRIKANER, BANTU and BRITON.

To me, as a schoolboy, these appeared, via not only van Jaarsveld but a multitude of subliminal messages from the outside world each day, to be the primary, if not exclusive, constituents of my environment. No doubt this vision was complicated by the presence of Coloureds and Indians, and a scattering of Others. But the perceived permanence of three major groups was accentuated in my case by a sharp sense of insecurity. Not only was my father in prison, but by association with him I was silently seen by my school-fellows to be politically tainted. And when he was released I knew we would be leaving: already the plug of place was loosened in my mind as the spiralling current of disappearance drew around us, threaded with old stories of exile of both the South African and Jewish variety.

What Dan Jacobson says of the British in Kimberley in his day remained pretty much true for Johannesburg in mine:

> There was no questioning that the dominant group in the city then, politically and culturally (and hence morally too), was the British. Whether colonial or 'home'-born, they ran the show; the latter among them especially. Somehow for *them* to have migrated to South Africa, however humble their circumstances might now be, was perceived by them (and others) almost as an act of *noblesse oblige*; for my parents to have done so, however, marked them down as 'foreigners'.[85]

If there were any potential nomads in my immediate surroundings, we were definitely amongst them. Most other

[85] *Heshel's Kingdom*, p.73

people living around us were as locked into place as the three groups in van Jaarsveld and van Wijk's diagram. Or seemed to be. At our high-school were the offspring of a considerable number of first or second generation immigrants, many of them from Mozambique, Portugal, Greece, Yugoslavia, Lebanon and Rhodesia. Other English-speaking high-schools in Johannesburg had even more diversity than we did. I wonder how many pupils, looking at the AFRIKANER, BANTU and BRITON trilogy, identified with the latter, as a result of origin, language, or wish for emulation of the cultural top-dogs.

Whatever each of us thought, there was a crushing pressure to conform, among adolescents in a white city with such a shallow social identity: after all, by the mid-1960's nobody over the age of eighty had actually been born in Johannesburg, since the city was only founded in 1886. There was so little white history linking us all to the place where we lived, and such a tenuous moral foothold available in the face of apartheid, that points of reference as clear as AFRIKANER, BRITON and BANTU seemed to be hewn out of everlasting rock. From the perspective of a high school student, it was virtually impossible to see how all three groups had themselves, at different times and in different ways, been involved in uncertain nomadic behaviour.

Yet South African history was and continues to be a driving, desperate, greedily bright-eyed, freewheeling, footloose tale of movement and the resistance to movement of many groups across wide spaces. It has been shaped, among others, by passing sailors and migrant armies, impis and ox-wagons, gold prospectors and diamond diggers, migrants and mercenaries, peddlers, raiders, refugees, exiles and insurgent guerrillas.

Writing in 1955, in the midst of the apartheid years, when political space was more deeply frozen than at any other, Dan Jacobson described South Africa as

> a multi-tongued nation of nomads[...] across a country too big and silent for us, too dry for cultivation, about which we went on roads like chains. We were caught within it, within this wide sad land we mined but did not cultivate.[86]

[86] *A Dance in the Sun*, pp.140,141

More recently, as the legal frontiers within the country have changed, as influx control has been abolished and the country has opened its borders to black Africa, this process has once more been set in full motion:

> All over South Africa, from north to south, masses of people are on the move, raising shacks as close as possible to the cities. They are looking for food or work or a little something to steal or some medicine for death. We are becoming more nomadic. The history of this country is a pattern of shifts and displacements, a raw war between settlers and disinherited.[87]

With hindsight, and with the wind of emigration in the soles of my shoes, it seems to me that Van Jaarsveld and Van Wijk's diagram, instead of representing a locked-in island, should show a wheel of many more than three spokes, buckled and punctured with its careening, creaking, ploughing, veering passage across the land.

Amnesia (Leaving home)

A woman visits a country in Eastern Europe, most likely Latvia, where her father came from a village of wooden houses and horse-drawn carts. He was Jewish, thirteen years old when he was sent off to South Africa, escaping a low-caste life and the approach of violent repression.

The woman never reaches this village, though in the opening paragraphs of the story she imagines how it might have been at the time of her father's leave-taking. On her own trip, in some other part of the country, she is witness to a pheasant hunt in a wood at dusk. The falling bird which strikes her on the shoulder brings home to her the fate which her father escaped:

> [...] the men with their thrashing sticks drive the prey racing on, rushing this way and that, no way where there are not men and sticks, men and guns. They have wings but dare not fly and reveal themselves, there was nowhere to run

[87] Breyten Breytenbach, *Return to Paradise*, p.12

to from the village to the fields as they came on and on, the kick of a cossack's mount ready to strike creeping heads, the thrust of a bayonet lifting a man by the heart like a piece of meat on a fork. Death advancing and nowhere to go.[88]

Later on the same page, the woman is left with nothing but this memory, and six leaves from the wood. The village is forgotten, but not the oppression:

> I didn't ask [my father] about his village. He never told me; or I wouldn't listen. I have the leaves in my hand. I did not know that I would find, here in the wood, the beaters advancing, advancing across the world.

This story by Nadine Gordimer, "My Father Leaves Home", is at least to some extent autobiographical. It is one of the few in which she writes of her Jewishness. Otherwise, she swings between effacement of this background in her fiction, and a sense of emptiness when asked about it in her interviews, as in this one with Margaret Walters:

> I didn't come from a family where I had been given Jewish religious upbringing or been taught anything about the history of Jewish people. I read it for myself when I grew up. I'm conscious of the fact that I'm Jewish, but it hasn't had anything much to do with the formation of my attitude to life, with my philosophy, or with my moral attitudes. For me, the formative thing has been being a white African.[89]

This statement is surprisingly flat for a writer with a fine sense of the multiplicity and inner tensions of her characters. Nor is it perhaps entirely accurate. In "My Father Leaves Home", the narrator, with a story not unlike Gordimer's own, has a horror of oppression that is directly linked to the story of her Jewish father.

But the actual relationship between this narrator and her father has an astringent taste to it. As a child in South Africa she shares her mother's disgust of his squalid past, and recoils

[88] NadineGordimer, "My Father Leaves Home", in *Jump*, p.66

[89] Margaret Walters, "Writers in Conversation", in Bazin and Seymour (eds.), *Conversations with Nadine Gordimer*, p.297

from the fear he provokes in his black servants. Everything about him, including his Jewishness, is diminished in her mind. And this corresponds to the way Gordimer speaks of her own father. "He just didn't have the guts to become much of a personality. There was something arrested about my father" she tells Jannika Hurwitt,[90] adding in an interview with Pippa Stein and Ruth Jacobson: "His attitude towards blacks was that they were beyond the human pale, an extraordinary attitude for someone who had fled from Tzarist oppression".[91]

It is oppression that Gordimer is sensitive to in the world around her. And in "My Father Leaves Home" she touches on the possibility that sensitivity might catch her so sharply by the throat at least partly because the root of her father's story is also her own.

In an Academic Freedom Lecture, directed against the racist Quota Act and delivered to a white student audience at Rhodes University in 1983, she herself uses the image of roots. Starting off by declaring herself to be

> the daughter of a man who couldn't get into high-school, in Lithuania,[92] under the quota for Jews set by the Russian Czar[93]

she later goes on to say that

> we whites have still to thrust the spade under the old roots of our lives [...] it is possible for whites to opt out of class and race privilege and identify with black liberation as their own liberation.[94]

What this sounds like is not only an act of abnegation involving a deep uprooting of the self, but at the same time an attempted grafting of that self onto someone else's tree. But is there not more to "the old roots of our lives" than "class and race privilege"?

---

[90] Jannika Hurwitt, "The Art of Fiction LXXVII: Nadine Gordimer", in Bazin and Seymour (eds.), *Conversations with Nadine Gordimer*, p.130

[91] Stein and Jacobson (eds.), *Sophiatown Speaks*, p. 26

[92] Gordimer's father came from a village outside Riga, in Latvia, not Lithuania. She repeats this error on several different occasions, for example in Stein and Jacobson (eds.), as above, p.25

[93] "Living in the Interregnum", Academic Freedom Lecture, Rhodes University, 1st September 1983, p.5

[94] pp.16, 17

I think back to Gordimer's early story, "Is There Nowhere Else Where We Can Meet?", which I looked at earlier in this book. There, the black man is identified with parts of the landscape, a cow, broken wood, fissured earth. The white woman who encounters him is in transit. As she tussles with him, she sees a bird, printed across the sky like a pure image of her own passage:

> Her face swung up and she saw the waves of a grey sky and a crane breasting them, beautiful as the figurehead of a ship.[95]

In "My Father Leaves Home", the very different and much older white woman escapes from the pheasant hunters in an Eastern European wood. The terrified birds turn into refugees from another time in her mind, her father could have been one of them had he stayed behind, she could be even now as one of them strikes her in its fall. She is also in transit, separated from the trees of the wood like a bird, like the six leaves she brings away from there and which she has in her hand at the end of the story.

She gathered them "for their pretty autumn stains," she is careful to say, "not out of any sentiment",[96] trying to burn a fire-break between herself and any emotion, though towards the end of "My Father Leaves Home" the narrator's emotion begins to rage.

The emotion comes from what she found in the wood, of fear in the present and her own past. It is also in the pushing away of her father. If this was as true for Gordimer as it is for her narrator, then perhaps both feelings drove her to dig the heels of her self more deeply into South Africa, distancing herself from her ancestral story. And even in South Africa itself, this was a dangerous story.

As early as 1902, the South African government passed anti-Semitic laws, the Immigration Restrictions Act being aimed chiefly at Indians and poverty-stricken Eastern European Jews. In 1930, seven years after Gordimer's birth, Jews were again the object of the Immigration Quota Act:

---

[95] "Is There Nowhere Else Where We Can Meet?" in *Selected Stories*, p.19

[96] "My Father Leaves Home", p.66

> This Act conclusively proved that Jews were finally fully acceptable to neither of the two main white population groups in South Africa. Six years later [D.F.] Malan […] leader of the Gesuiwerde Nasionale Party Opposition and Prime Minister in 1948, demanded at his party's congress in November 1936 both the halting of all German-Jewish immigration, and disabling legislation against Jews already in the country.[97]

This is not part of the history traced by Gordimer in her fiction, which throws light on Black, Afrikaner and Briton, immigrant settlers of all kinds but almost never her own. Would it be unfair to say there is a kind of amnesia involved here? Would a degree of forgetting be the necessary price for the survival of the writer so strongly drawn to the environment she grew up in, its beauty balanced against deep injustice? Is this the first generation Jewish South African who must draw a veil across her own past to truly enter the present? How many like her turned to a fiercely rational humanism, wanting to leave behind them the old religious forms as well as the spiritual touchstone, but also the raw-nerved vulnerability and uncertain roadmap of Jewishness?

> being Jewish […]
> a silence, an absence, a question,
> a self-questioning, a vagueness, an anxiety:
>
> an anxious certitude,
> behind which lies another certitude,
> abstract, heavy, unbearable:
> that of being designated as Jewish […]
>
> […]
>
> Somewhere, I am a stranger in relation to something of myself […][98]

I write this from France, more than thirty years after leaving South Africa. The phrase "My father leaves home" has by now gathered multiple gritty layers of meaning to it in my mind. From

[97] Joseph Sherman, Introduction to *From a Far Off Land*, p.3

[98] Georges Perec, *Ellis Island*, pp.58, 59

my own father leaving home, to both my parents' fathers leaving home at different points and for different reasons, leaving their children behind.

And though I live with my children, I too have left several homes, not least of all those surrounded by the English language. It was not so long ago that I went to tuck my daughter in and wished her sweet dreams, in French. "Fais de belles rêves", I said. Instead of sighing gently into her pillow she opened her eyes in weary consternation and corrected the gender of the adjective, which should have been "beaux".

Our children will always know that I am not entirely at home. Against the vulnerability of this state I have, apart from family and friends, the act of reading and writing. And a memory like the one Gordimer sets out in the opening paragraphs of her story, a bag of stones to strew behind me, concerning the rites and passages of my own and those who came before me, to come to where I am.

"My father leaves home" means to me that there will always be a track going off to another place, a dream or a need or a terrible imperative. There will always be a gap between father and land, as between mother and tongue, home and traveller, the walls of before and the door to the future. And this is my breathing space, my footloose disappearing point, the place between places that these words come from.

ACKNOWLEDGEMENTS

My thanks to Jon Cook, not only for the paths he suggested I explore further in this writing, but for his unusually acute and creative listening power. I walked into his office at the University of East Anglia in Norwich and tried to persuade him that, even if I needed a doctorate for professional reasons, I should not try and get one. I told him that I did not type. That I worked slowly. That I did not have e-mail. That I was not interested in further academic studies. All these things, at that time, were true. He did not bat an eyelid, but sat there intently listening to me. I can't remember what else I said. At some point his wife phoned; she was having car trouble and wanted advice. I looked around the office, with books up to the ceiling and papers on the floor. Then he put down the phone and went on listening.

For three years he listened, month after month, picking up on ideas behind my ideas, landmarks beyond my line of sight, silences at the heart of my words. In its original form, *White Scars* was officially the "reflective and critical" component to my doctorate in "creative writing". With John Cook responding to my various drafts, it became a journey. But he bears no responsibility for these pages, which are my own doing and have considerably and in places radically altered since he last saw them as my thesis advisor.

Thanks to Robert Berold, Stephen Clingman and Isobel Dixon for their meticulous and creative reading of the manuscript, all of them helping me transform it into its present form, especially in those last fiercely delicate weeks before this book went to print.

Thanks also to Ansie Cilliers for her careful revision of my Breytenbach translations.

BIBLIOGRAPHY OF CITED WORKS

Achebe, Chinua, "African Literature as Celebration", *Dissent*, Summer 1992, pp. 344-351.

Afshar, Haleh, "Talk on Baruch Hirson at the Institute of Commonwealth Studies, London, 14th October 2000", in Denis Hirson (ed.), *In Memory of Baruch Hirson* (London: Private printing, 2003).

Amichai, Yehuda, *Open Closed Open* (New York: Harcourt, 2000).

Aurelius, Marcus, *Meditations* (London: Penguin, 1969).

Banoobhai, Shabbir, *echoes of my other self* (Johannesburg: Ravan, 1980).

Bazin, Nancy Topping and Seymour, Marilyn Dallman (eds.), *Conversations with Nadine Gordimer* (Jackson: University Press of Mississippi, 1990).

Beier, Ulli (ed.), *An Introduction to African Literature* (London: Longman, 1967).

Bellos, David, *Georges Perec, une vie dans les mots* (Paris: Le Seuil, 1994).

Berger, John, "The Culture of Arrival", in *"The Guardian"*, 12 October 2002, p.14.

Berold, Robert, "On Editing a Poetry Magazine", *Comment* , 10, Summer 1992, pp. 6-8.

Berold, Robert, (ed.), *South African Poets on Poetry* (Durban: Gecko Poetry, 2003).

Bertelli, Dominique and Ribière, Mireille (eds.), *Georges Perec, entretiens et conferences, Volume I, 1965-1978* (Nantes: Joseph K., 2003).

Bertelli, Dominique and Ribière, Mireille (eds.), *Georges Perec, entretiens et conferences, Volume 2, 1979-1981* (Nantes: Joseph K., 2003).

Boetie, Dugmore, *Familiarity is the Kingdom of the Lost* (London: Barrie & Rockliff: The Cresset Press, 1969).

Bogin, Nina, *The Winter Orchards* (London: Anvil Press, 2001).

Bosman, D.B., van der Merwe, I.W., Hiemstra, M.A., *Tweetalige Woordeboek* (Cape Town: Tafelberg, 1975).

Brainard, Joe, *I Remember (Je me souviens)* (Arles: Actes Sud, 1997).

Brainard, Joe, *I Remember* (New York: Granary Books, 2001).

Brasseur, Roland, *Je me souviens de Je me souviens* (Paris: Le

Castor Astrale, 1998).
Bremner, Lindsay, "Crime and the Emerging Landscape of Post-Apartheid Johannesburg ", in Judin, Hilton and Vladislavic, Ivan (eds.), *Architecture, Apartheid and After* (Rotterdam: Nai Publishers, 1998).
Breytenbach, Breyten, *Het Huis van de Dove (Collected Poems 1964–1969)* (Amsterdam: Meulenhoff, 1976).
Breytenbach, Breyten, *Feu froid* (Paris: Christian Bourgois, 1977).
Breytenbach, Breyten, *In Africa Even the Flies are Happy* (Selected Poems 1964- 1977) (London: John Calder, 1978).
Breytenbach, Breyten, *A Season in Paradise* (London: Jonathan Cape, 1980).
Breytenbach, Breyten, "Propos Détenus", afterword to *Feu froid* (Paris: Christian Bourgois, 1983).
Breytenbach, Breyten, *The True Confessions of an Albino Terrorist* (London: Faber and Faber, 1984).
Breytenbach, Breyten, *Notes of Bird* (Amsterdam : Meulenhoff, 1984).
Breytenbach, Breyten, *End Papers* (New York: Farrar, Strauss and Giroux, 1986).
Breytenbach, Breyten, *Hovering Dog* (Prison Poems 1975–1982) (unpublished M.S., 1986).
Breytenbach, Breyten, *Judas Eye* (London: Faber and Faber, 1988).
Breyten Breytenbach, *Painting the Eye* (Cape Town: David Philip, 1993).
Breytenbach, Breyten, *Return to Paradise* (Cape Town: David Philip, 1993).
Carver, Raymond, *Cathedral* (New York: Vintage Books, 1984).
Carver, Raymond, *Fires* (London: Picador, 1986).
Carver, Raymond, *In a Marine Light* (London: Picador, 1988).
Carver, Raymond, *Where I'm Calling From* (London: The Harvill Press, 1993).
Carver, Raymond, *All of Us* (London: The Harvill Press, 1997).
Chaix, Marie, Preface to Brainard, Joe, *I Remember (Je me souviens)* (Arles: Actes Sud, 1997).
Coetzee, J.M., *Waiting for the Barbarians* (Johannesburg: Ravan

Press, 1981).
De Kok, Ingrid, *Familiar Ground* (Johannesburg: Ravan Press, 1988).
Dictionary of South African English (New York: Oxford University Press, 1996).
Gallagher, Tess, Introduction to Carver, Raymond, *A New Path to the Waterfall*, 1989, in Carver, Raymond, *All of Us* (London: The Harvill Press, 1997).
Gallagher, Tess, Introduction to Raymond Carver's *All of Us* (London: The Harvill Press, 1997).
Gaucher, Mgr. Guy, *Sainte Thérèse de Lisieux* (Strasbourg: Editions du Signe, 1994).
Gentry, Marshall Bruce and Stull, William L. (eds.), *Conversations with Raymond Carver* (Jackson: University Press of Mississippi, 1990).
Gordimer, Nadine, *Selected Stories* (London: Penguin, 1983).
Gordimer, Nadine, "Living in the Interregnum", Academic Freedom Lecture, Rhodes University, 1 September 1983 (typescript).
Gordimer, Nadine, *Jump and Other Stories* (London: Bloomsbury, 1991).
Gwala, Mafika Pascal, *Jol'iinkomo* (Johannesburg: Ad. Donker, 1977).
Halpert, Sam (ed.), *Raymond Carver, an Oral Biography* (Iowa City: University of Iowa Press, 1995).
Hirson, Baruch, *Year of Fire, Year of Ash* (London: Zed Books, 1979).
Hirson, Baruch, *Revolutions in my Life* (Johannesburg: Witwatersrand University Press, 1995).
Hirson, Denis, *The House Next Door to Africa* (Cape Town: David Philip, 1986).
Hirson, Denis with Trump, Martin (eds.), *The Heinemann Book of South African Short Stories* (Oxford: Heinemann, 1994).
Hirson, Denis (ed.), *The Lava of this Land, South African Poetry 1960-1996* (Evanston: TriQuarterly Books/Northwestern University Press, 1997).
Hirson, Denis, "Gardening in the Dark" in *New Coin* Vol.6 No.2, Dec. 2000, pp.38-44.

Hirson, Denis (ed.), *In Memory of Baruch Hirson* (Private printing: London, 2003).
Hirson, Denis, *I Remember King Kong (the Boxer)* (Johannesburg: Jacana, 2004).
Hirson, Yael, *A Story for Anna* (unpublished, 2004).
Jacobson, Dan, *The Trap* and *A Dance in the Sun* (Cape Town: David Philip, 1985 (1955)).
Jacobson, Dan, *Heshel's Kingdom* (London: Penguin, 1999).
Jensma, Wopko, *i must show you my clippings* (Johannesburg: Ravan Press, 1977).
Jonker, Ingrid, *Selected Poems* (Cape Town: Human and Rousseau, 1988).
Joyce, James, *A Portrait of the Artist as a Young Man* (New York: The Viking Press, 1971 (1916)).
Jurgenson, Luba, *L'expérience concentrationnaire est-elle indicible?* (Paris: Editions du Rocher, 2003).
Kavanagh, Robert and Qangule, Z.S. (eds.), *The Making of a Servant* (Johannesburg: Ophir-Ravan, 1974).
Krog, Antjie, *Untitled film interview with Denis Hirson* (Cape Town, 1995).
Krog, Antjie, *Country of my Skull* (Johannesburg: Random House, 1998).
Krog, Antjie, *Down to my Last Skin* (Johannesburg: Random House, 2000).
Kuper, Leo, *Passive Resistance in South Africa* (London: Jonathan Cape, 1956).
Lewin, Hugh, *Bandiet* (London: Barrie and Jenkins, 1974).
Lewin, Hugh, *Bandiet out of Jail* (Johannesburg: Random House, 2002).
Mathews, Harry, *The Orchard* (Flint: Bamberger Books, 1988).
Matshikiza, Todd, *Chocolates for my Wife* (Cape Town: David Philip, 1982 (1961)).
Milosz, Czeslaw, *Bells in Winter* (Manchester: Carcanet Press, 1982).
Mphahlele, Es'kia, "Black and White" in *New Statesman*, 10th Sept. 1960, pp. 342-346.
Mphahlele, Es'kia, *Down Second Avenue* (London: Faber, 1971 (1959)).

Mthimkulu, Oupa Thando, "Like a Wheel" in *Staffrider* Vol. 1 No.1 1978, p.21.
Mthimkulu, Oupa Thando, *Out of Africa into Exile* (typescript, 1995).
Mtshali, Oswald, *Sounds of a Cowhide Drum* (Johannesburg, Renoster Books, 1971).
Ndebele, Njabulo, *The Rediscovery of the Ordinary* (Johannesburg: COSAW, 1991).
Nkosi, Lewis, "Fiction by Black South Africans", in Beier, Ulli (ed.), *An Introduction to African Literature* (London: Longman, 1967).
Opperman, D.J. (ed.), *Groot Verseboek* (Cape Town: Tafelberg, 1990).
Padgett, Ron, Afterword to Brainard, Joe, *I Remember* (New York: Granary Books, 2001).
Pampallis, John, *Foundations of the New South Africa* (London: Zed Books, 1991).
Paton, Alan, *Debbie Go Home* (London: Penguin, 1968 (1961)).
Perec, Georges, *Les choses* (Paris: Presses Pocket/Julliard, 1988 (1965)).
Perec, Georges, *La boutique obscure* (Paris; Denoël, 1988 (1973)).
Perec, Georges, *L'infra-ordinaire* (Paris: Seuil, 1989).
Perec, Georges, *Je suis né* (Paris: Seuil, 1990).
Perec, Georges, *La disparition* (Paris: Gallimard, 1991 (1969)).
Perec, Georges, *Je me souviens* (Paris: Hachette/P.O.L, (1998 (1978)).
Perec, Georges, *Ellis Island* (Paris: P.O.L., 1999 (1980)).
Perec, Georges, *Espèces d'espaces* (Paris: Galilée, 2000 (1974)).
Perec, Georges, *W ou le souvenir d'enfance* (Paris: Denoël, 2002 (1975)).
Perec, Paulette, "Chronique de la vie de Georges Perec", in Paulette Perec (ed.), *Portrait(s) de Georges Perec* (Paris: Bibliothèque nationale de France, 2001).
Plaatje, Sol.T., *Native Life in South Africa* (Johannesburg: Ravan, 1982 (1916)).
Press, Karen, "Tiresias in the City of Heroes", in *Home* (Manchester: Carcanet, 2000).
Reeves, Ambrose, *Shooting at Sharpeville* (London: Victor

Gollancz, 1960).
Rose, Steven, *The Making of Memory* (London: Bantam, 1993).
Serote, Mongane Wally, *To Every Birth its Blood* (Johannesburg: Ravan Press, 1981).
Serote, Mongane Wally, *Yakhal'inkomo* (Johannesburg: Ad. Donker, 1983 (1972)).
Sherman, Joseph, Introduction to Sherman, Joseph (ed.), *From a Land Far Off* (Cape Town: Jewish Publications – South Africa, 1987).
Sole, Kelwyn, *Projections in the Past Tense* (Johannesburg: Ravan Press, 1992).
Sontag, Susan, *Regarding the Pain of Others* (New York: Picador, 2003).
Stein, Pippa and Jacobson, Ruth (eds.), *Sophiatown Speaks* (Johannesburg: Junction Avenue Press, 1986).
Turner, Victor W., *The Ritual Process* (London: Penguin, 1974).
Van Gennep, Arnold, *The Rites of Passage* (London: Routledge and Kegan Paul, 1977 (1960)).
Van Jaarsveld, F.A. and van Wijk, Theo, *Illustrated History for Senior Certificates Stds. IX and X* (Johannesburg: Voortrekkerspers, 1965 (1961)).
"Verwoerd Gives Riot Details", in *The Cape Times*, 22nd March 1960, p.1.
Virilio, Paul, "Un homme qui marche", in Perec, Paulette (ed.), *Portrait(s) de Georges Perec* (Paris: Bibliothéque nationale de France, 2001).
Walcott, Derek, "Near Felicity, Listening to the Rain on a Statue's Forehead", in *The International Herald Tribune*, 10th December, 1992, p.9.
Walker, Eric A., *A History of Southern Africa* (London: Longmans, 1959).
Williams, Raymond, *Keywords* (London: HarperCollins, 1988 (1976)).

PERMISSIONS

The publishers would like to thank the following people and agencies for permission to use quotes and extracts:

AM Heath: Dan Jacobson, *A Trap* and *A Dance in the Sun* (Cape Town: David Philip, 1985); and Dan Jacobson, *Heshel's Kingdom* (London: Penguin, 1999)

Anvil Press Poetry: Nina Bogin, "There's No Hour" in *The Winter Orchards* (London: The Winter Orchards, 2001)

A P Watt Ltd: Nadine Gordimer, "Is There Nowhere Else We Can Meet?" in *The Soft Voice Of The Serpent* (London: Penguin, 1983); Nadine Gordimer, transcript of the Academic Freedom Lecture "Living In The Interregnum", given at Rhodes University in 1983; Jannika Hurwitt interview with Nadine Gordimer "The Art of Fiction LXXVII: Nadine Gordimer", in Nancy Topping Bazin and Marilyn Dallman Seymour (eds), *Conversations with Nadine Gordimer* (Jackson: University Press of Mississippi, 1990). Originally in the *Paris Review*, 88 (Summer 1983), pp.82–127; Stein, Pippa and Jacobson, Ruth (eds.), *Sophiatown Speaks* (Johannesburg: Junction Avenue Press, 1986); Margaret Walters, transcript of interview "Writers in conversation: Nadine Gordimer" ICA Video: Writer's Talk #62, The Roland Collection

Bibliothéque nationale de France: Paulette Perec ed. *Portrait(s) de Georges Perec* (Paris: Bibliothéque nationale de France, 2001)

Bloomsbury: Nadine Gordimer, "My Father Leaves Home" in *Jump and Other Stories* (London: Bloomsbury, 1991)

Breyten Breytenbach: Breyten Breytenbach, *Painting the Eye* (Cape Town: David Philip, 1993); Breyten Breytenbach, *Return to Paradise* (Cape Town: David Philip, 1993); Breyten Breytenbach, "on paper" in *Judas Eye* (London: Faber and Faber, 1988); Breyten Breytenbach, "Journey (: I have Died a Little)" in *In Africa Even The Flies Are Happy* (London: John Calder, 1978). Originally "Reis (:ek 'n bietjie dood)" in *'n Seisoen in die Paradys* (Johannesburg: Perskor-Uitgewer, 1976); and Breyten Breytenbach, *Notes of Bird* (Amsterdam: Meulenhoff, 1984)

Carcanet Press Limited: Czeslaw Milosz, "Ars Poetica" in *Bells in Winter* (Manchester: Carcanet Press, 1982); and Karen Press, "Tiresias in the City of Heroes" in *Home* (Manchester: Carcanet, 2000)

Editions du Seuil: L'infra-ordinaire by Georges Perec © Editions du Seuil, 1989, Collection La Librairie du XX1e siecle directed by Maurice Olender

Editions Galilée: Georges Perec, *Espèces d'espaces*, copyright Editions Galilée, 1974-2000

Farrar, Strauss and Giroux: Breyten Breytenbach, *End Papers* (New York: Farrar, Strauss and Giroux, 1986)

Frances Bond: Alan Paton, "A Drink in the Passage" in *Debbie Go Home* (London: Penguin Books, 1961)

Georges Borchardt, Inc. (on behalf of Chana Bloch and Chana Kronfeld): Yehuda Amichai, *Open Closed Open* (New York: Harcourt, 2000). Compilation Copyright © 2000 by Yehuda Amichai. English Translation Copyright © 2000 by Chana Block and Chana Kronfeld.

Hachette Littératures: Georges Perec, *Je me souviens* (Paris: Hachette/P.O.L., 1998 [1978])

Harry Mathews: Harry Mathews, *The Orchard* (Flint: Bamberger Books, 1988)

Hugh Lewin: Hugh Lewin, "Pylon" in *Bandiet out of Jail* (Johannesburg: Random House, 2002)

International Creative Management, Inc: Raymond Carver, *In a Marine Light* (London: Picador, 1988); *Cathedral* (New York: Vintage Books, 1984); *Fires* (London: Picador, 1986); *Where I'm Calling From* (London: The Harvill Press, 1993); *All of Us* (London: The Harvill Press, 1997); Tess Gallagher, Introductions to Raymond Carver's *A New Path to the Waterfall*, and *All of Us*, both in Raymond Carver, *All of Us* (London: The Harvill Press, 1997)

Jonathan Ball Publishers: Wally Mongane Serote, "Alexandra" in *Yakhal'inkomo* (Johannesburg: Ad. Donker, 1983); and Motshile wa Nthodi, "South Africa Dialogue" in *A Century of South African Poetry* ed. Mike Chapman (Johannesburg: Ad. Donker, 1981)

Joseph Sherman: Joseph Sherman, Introduction to *From a Land Far Off*, ed. Joseph Sherman (Cape Town: Jewish Publications, 1987)

Kelwyn Sole: Kelwyn Sole, "The National Question" in *Projections in the Past Tense* (Johannesburg: Ravan Press, 1992)

NB Publishers: Bartho Smit, *Ek Vat My Land* in *Huisgenoot* (1951) and in the anthology *Bolder*, ed. Hennie Aucamp (publisher and page reference unknown). This translation into English in Denis Hirson with Martin Trump eds. *The Heinemann Book of South African Short Stories,* (Oxford: Heinemann, 1994). Breyten Breytenbach, *Die Ysterkoei Moet Sweet* (Johannesburg: Afrikaanse pers-boekhandel, 1964): "provisional fulfilment" (originally "voorlopige vorvulling"); "headtrip from fear to seed" (originally "kopreis van vrees tot saad,"); "log-book" (originally "dagboek"); "listen the raw season" (originally "luister die rou seisoen"); "only for you this pulsing summer fruit" (originally "net vir jou dié polsende somervrug"); "writing now and from back to front" (originally "skrywende nou en van agter tot voor"); and "ordain" (originally "wy"). Breyten Breytenbach, *In Africa Even The Flies Are Happy* (London: John Calder, 1978): "Exile Representative" (originally "Balling, verteenwoordiger" in *Skryt*, [Amsterdam: Meulenhoff, 1972]); "co la" (originally "co la" in *Die Ysterkoei Moet Sweet* (Johannesburg: Afrikaanse pers-boekhandel, 1964); and "The Threat of the Sick" (originally "bedreiging van die siektes") in *Die Ysterkoei Moet Sweet* (Afrikaanse pers-boekhandel). Breyten Breytenbach, *True Confessions of an Albino Terrorist* (Johannesburg: Taurus, 1984); and "The Struggle for the Taal", in *True Confessions of an Albino Terrorist*, Taurus. Breyten Breytenbach *A Season in Paradise* (London: Jonathan Cape, 1980). Ingrid Jonker, "The Child Who Was Shot Dead by Soldiers in Nyanga" in *Selected Poems* (Cape Town: Human and Rousseau, 1988). Wilma Stockenström, "Housebreaking of the Mamba". This translation in Denis Hirson ed. *The Lava of this Land* (Evanston: Northwestern University Press, 1997). Original poem in *Vir die Bysiende Leser* (Cape Town: Human and Rousseau, 1970)

Pan MacMillan: Wally Serote, *To Every Birth its Blood* (Johannesburg: Ravan Press, 1981)

P.O.L.: Ellis Island © P.O.L. 1995: Georges Perec, *Ellis Island* (Paris: P.O.L., 1999 [1980])

Random House: Breyten Breytenbach, *A Season In Paradise* (London: Jonathan Cape, 1980)

Robert Berold: Robert Berold, "On Editing a Poetry Magazine", Comment, 10, Summer 1992

Shabbir Banoobhai: Shabbir Bhanoobhai, "the border" in *echoes of my other self* (Johannesburg: Ravan Press, 1980)

The Baruch Hirson Estate: Baruch Hirson, *Year of Fire, Year of Ash* (London: Zed Books, 1979); and Baruch Hirson, *Revolutions in my Life* (Johannesburg: Witwatersrand University Press, 1995)

The Joe Brainard Estate: Joe Brainard, *I Remember (Je me souviens)* (Arles: Actes Sud, 1997); and *I Remember* (New York: Granary Books, 2001)

The University of Iowa Press: *Raymond Carver, an Oral Biography*, ed. Sam Halpert (Iowa City: University of Iowa Press, 1995)

The Wopko Jensma Estate: Wopko Jensma, "Spanner in the What? Works" in *i must show you my clippings* (Johannesburg, Ravan Press, 1977)

Yael Hirson: Yael Hirson, *A Story for Anna* (unpublished, 2004)

The publishers have endeavoured to trace all sources and obtain relevant permission. In the case of omission, or if we have been unable to trace the published sources of quotes, please contact the publisher at the address below to rectify any outstanding matters:

Jacana Media (Pty) Ltd
10 Orange Street
Sunnyside
Auckland Park 2092
South Africa

Other Titles by Jacana Media

I Remember King Kong (The Boxer) – Denis Hirson

We Walk Straight So You Better Get Out the Way
– Denis Hirson

A People on the Boil – Harry Mashabela

Globalisation and New Identities: A View from the Middle
– edited by Peter Alexander, Marcelle Dawson and Meera Ichharam

Operation Vula – Conny Braam

A Free Mind: Ahmed Kathrada's Notebook from Robben Island
– edited by Sahm Venter

Mr Chameleon – Tatamkhulu Afrika

See a complete list of Jacana titles at www.jacana.co.za